CHRIST
IN THE
Class
room

"With this innovative and exciting new book, Jared Dees embraces the ancient practice of lectio divina as a dynamic framework for faith lessons your students will never forget—and encounters with Christ that will transform their lives."

Lisa Mladinich
Founder of AmazingCatechists.com

"Jared Dees is the encouraging mentor every catechist and religion teacher needs. In *Christ in the Classroom*, we discover ways to not only assist students in learning more about Christ but also, more significantly, to provide frequent opportunities for students to meet him."

Pat Gohn
Editor of *Catechist* and author of *All In*

"As a director of religious education for the last forty-five years, I am absolutely convinced that Jared Dees is spot on with this approach."

Peggy Pigors
Coordinator of Adult Faith Formation at St. Clare Parish
Santa Clarita, California

"Lectio divina lesson planning is an awesome catechetical method. Since I teach every day, I cannot thank Jared Dees enough for this priceless approach."

Gerri Jose
Master Catechist at St. Elizabeth Parish
San Francisco, California

CHRIST
IN THE
Class
room

Lesson Planning for the Heart and Mind

JARED DEES

AVE MARIA PRESS   AVE   Notre Dame, Indiana

© 2018 by Jared Dees

All rights reserved. No part of this book may be used or reproduced in any manner whatsoever, except in the case of reprints in the context of reviews, without written permission from Ave Maria Press®, Inc., P.O. Box 428, Notre Dame, IN 46556, 1-800-282-1865.

Founded in 1865, Ave Maria Press is a ministry of the United States Province of Holy Cross.

www.avemariapress.com

Paperback: ISBN-13 978-1-59471-861-8

E-book: ISBN-13 978-1-59471-862-5

Cover and text design by Andy Wagoner.

Printed and bound in the United States of America

Library of Congress Cataloging-in-Publication Data is available.

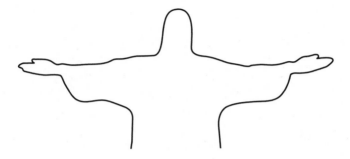

To Jen and our girls,
Addie, Anna, Francie, and Maggie,
who teach me every day how to love.

CONTENTS

INTRODUCTION

"The Gospel of the Lord," the bishop proclaimed. "Praise to you, Lord Jesus Christ," the eighth-graders responded. This was their time. I knew they were ready. Our bishop began his homily just as he had done the year before. He said a few words about the Holy Spirit, then walked from the ambo toward the group of eighth-graders about to receive the sacrament of Confirmation. I was their catechist. I had prepared them for this day, and I knew what was about to happen.

A year earlier, this same bishop presided over the Confirmations in our parish for the first time. Like a lot of bishops during Confirmation Masses, he quizzed the confirmandi to see how much they had learned. He asked questions about Pentecost, the gifts and fruits of the Holy Spirit, and the Trinity. He asked many questions, but he got very few responses. I was sad to see the disappointment on our bishop's face. I had decided then that I would not let the same thing happen again.

As soon as I got home that night, I wrote down every question I could remember the bishop asking my eighth-grade students. I was determined to prepare my next class for that homily. They would know the answers. They would have hands raised and responses ready. I was on a mission! It just wasn't the right mission.

A year later, our bishop began his homily, and I was confident in my students' ability to perform. He asked many of the same questions as he had the previous year, and I was proud to see my students raise their hands. They were ready. They had the answers. Mission accomplished. Or was it?

I did not leave that Mass satisfied with what I had done with those students. I left, instead, with a feeling of unrest even worse than the year before. They knew the answers to the bishop's questions, but did they grasp the significance of what they had just experienced? They could name the gifts and fruits of the Holy Spirit, but were their hearts open and prepared to accept those gifts as graces of the sacrament and put them to work in their daily lives?

I realized that year that I had been approaching religious education all wrong. I was focused almost exclusively on the head and not the heart. I was preparing my students to understand ideas and perform well on tests and quizzes. I set lesson objectives each day with goals for my students to learn *about* God—but I didn't set goals and objectives to encourage them to *love* God.

TYPICAL RELIGIOUS EDUCATION

When we first step foot into our classrooms, we religion teachers and catechists aim to make an impact. We want to inspire young people to embrace the faith and learn more about God. Our hopes and dreams, however, tend to quickly bump up against the challenges of planning and executing engaging lessons that touch both the head and the heart.

Like a lot of religious educators, when I first started out, I defaulted to a standard form of education. I started teaching the way I was taught. I did things as I thought they had always been done—in ways that seemed to make good sense. As a result, I made some big mistakes in my first years of teaching, and I suspect you have also made some of these.

MISTAKE #1: LONG LECTURES

My college and even high-school experience was pretty typical: long lectures and lots of notes. When I became a middle-school teacher for the first time,

I just assumed this was how students learn best. I found, however, that long lectures do not work.

I talked for extended periods and expected my students to sit quietly and take notes. Note taking amounted to copying verbatim what I was saying, writing on the board, or showing on my Power-Point. The students, of course, were not able to listen attentively for very long. They were bored no matter how interesting I thought my lecture was.

The worst part was that I was exhausted. I was preparing six lessons and lectures each day, which required my reading and comprehending a lot of material. The students were tired, too, but not from working hard. They were tired from the boredom of being asked only to listen.

I didn't have a clear understanding of what effective education could be. I didn't realize the power of leading rather than lecturing. I was not giving my students activities and assignments that inspired curiosity and connection. I was just asking them to listen and remember. Their hearts were not into it and, frankly, neither were their heads.

MISTAKE #2: READ AND REVIEW

Part of the challenge for me was a lack of resources. Most of us are given only a textbook when we first start out. So what else is there to do but read it, right?

I spent way too much time in my early years having students read aloud from the textbook and then assigning review questions in the book as homework. We read in class because I did not trust them to do so at home and remember everything the next day.

The first problem with this approach is limited class engagement. When students take turns reading aloud, it's likely that only one student in the entire class is fully engaged. Only one student is reading while the rest are supposed to be listening. Often the scene unfolds this way: When the first student finishes reading, you call on another student who has lost his place on the page. "We are on the fourth paragraph on page 47," you say, but still he can't seem to find the right spot. Then he starts reading and—forgive him, he is still very young—reads so slowly that the rest of the class has a hard time following along.

The second problem with this approach is lack of relevance for the students in what they read. They come away with a vague understanding of important topics and definitions, but none of it matters to them. They don't see why this lesson is important to their lives right now, and therefore, they quickly forget what they read.

Finally, like a lot of other educators, I kept the kids accountable by assigning the review questions at the end of each section we read. They answered the questions in complete sentences either in class or as homework. I occasionally checked for under-standing, but mostly I was just checking for partici-pation. I wanted to make sure they read the textbook. Unfortunately, I was not as focused on helping them do something with what they read as I should have been. I didn't help them bridge the gap between what they read and how they lived their lives.

MISTAKE #3: BUSYWORK

I'll never forget the time our principal walked into my classroom during my first year of teaching and asked me what the students were working on. "Busywork," I said without thinking. You should have seen the look on her face. "*What?!,*" she asked. "Oh—uh—I mean, they are completing a work-sheet. It's about something we just talked about. It's important work."

I don't remember what assignment they were working on, but it probably was just busywork. That is, it was likely something I assigned to give myself a break from all the lecturing I was doing. I'm sure I found a crossword puzzle or textbook handout to give to the students that matched up to what I was teaching.

Teachers sometimes assign busywork to keep kids quiet and even entertained, but that does not necessarily mean they are engaged. The students may work diligently on that word search or coloring sheet that you selected, but are they any closer to Christ because of it?

Religious educators must find worksheets and resources that challenge students and help them make connections to their daily lives. When you search online for a worksheet to use in class, do you take time to consider whether it will teach your students anything? Will it challenge them to think? Will it guide them to reflect on something they learned? Will it require your help and give you the opportunity to clarify some important idea about our faith? Find resources that challenge your students to think and make connections between what they have learned and how they live their everyday lives.

FROM IDEAS TO ENCOUNTER

These mistakes all stem from the problem at the root of my understanding of teaching. I was optimizing only for an education of ideas. I was trying to pass on a way of thinking about Catholicism, but I was missing something very important. What I should have done—what we all need to do as religious educators—is optimize for an education of encounter.

In his encyclical *Deus Caritas Est*, Pope Benedict XVI wrote, "Being Christian is not the result of an ethical choice or a lofty idea, but the encounter with an event, a person, which gives life a new horizon and a decisive direction" (1). If that is the case, then everything we do as religious educators should have a simple goal: an encounter with Christ.

An education of encounter guides students to meet Jesus for themselves. As a result of that meeting, the students are transformed, usually in small but sometimes in big ways. We still introduce and explain ideas about faith, but only to prepare our students with the understanding necessary to meet God themselves.

Our goal goes beyond the head; we must also engage the heart. An education of encounter seeks to instruct students in what we believe and also to open their hearts so they can make those beliefs their own. We seek to teach the head so Christ can touch the heart. Our job is to lead our students into an encounter with Christ, who has the power to transform their lives.

Through constant encounters with the love of Christ, students will become lifelong learners under our care. They will be disciples of Christ, learning everything they can about him so that they can live more like him. As a result, they will reflect that love for others by showing them how to find that love for themselves.

A SOLUTION STUDYING SCRIPTURE

In 2013, I was developing a set of worksheets for my website, *The Religion Teacher*, to help religion teachers and catechists teach students how to use the Bible. I wanted to create templates that could be easily printed and distributed. The problem was that I didn't have a structure or framework for these worksheets that would make them effective tools for handing on the faith to students.

Then it hit me: lectio divina. *Lectio divina*, which is Latin for "sacred reading," is a process by which we encounter Christ through reading scripture with the help of the Holy Spirit. We meditate on God's Word and respond to Christ in prayer. This seemed to be the perfect process to use to create catechetical resources on reading the Bible.

Lectio divina, however, has been described in so many different ways over the years. It seemed as though no two people had the same way of explaining it. I had experienced the practice most often at the direction of Jesuit priests I knew personally or found online. It was a wonderful way to read the Bible, but how could I replicate the guidance I had received in the tools I wanted to create for religious educators?

After some research, I stumbled upon what would become for me, at first, a new way of reading the Bible and then later a new way to teach everything about the Catholic faith. It came in Pope Benedict XVI's postsynodal apostolic exhortation *Verbum Domini*. In that document, the Holy Father reviewed the basic steps of lectio divina and added simple questions tailored to each phase of this approach to sacred reading:

1. Reading (lectio): What does the biblical text say in itself?

2. Meditation (meditatio): What does the biblical text say to us?

3. Prayer (oratio): What can I say to the Lord in response to his Word?

4. Contemplation (contemplatio): What conversion of the mind, heart, and life is the Lord asking of us?

According to Pope Benedict XVI, what follows the activity of sacred reading is a fifth step that shows how our lives have been transformed into action (actio). Actio "moves the believer to make his or her life a gift for others in charity" (*VD*, 87).

After I discovered Pope Benedict XVI's approach to lectio divina, I started applying it to my own daily prayer practice. I had been reading the daily Mass readings each morning, but I wasn't doing much more than that. I wasn't praying with scripture. This simple process, which is so easy to remember, led me to consider what the text was saying to me on the day I was reading it and how I should respond to God in prayer. It helped me discern those changes in my life, both big and small, that were most needed each day.

At the same time, I started to apply this approach to the resources I was creating at *The Religion Teacher*. I now had a simple system—a pedagogy of the Word if you will—that I could implement in the creation of teaching tools. These resources have helped hundreds of teachers guide their students toward achieving not only reading comprehension but also contemplation of how God's Word might truly matter in their lives.

As you will discover in this book, I now see these four steps and their four corresponding questions to be fruitful well beyond the study of God's Word revealed in scripture. They also form a process through which we can encounter the Word of God in the entire deposit of faith, both sacred scripture and sacred tradition. Indeed, this process can and should be used in the way we organize every approach to catechesis and faith formation because it enables us to inspire both the heads and the hearts of the students we teach.

LESSON PLANNING WITH LECTIO IN MIND

It was not long after I started using lectio divina to lead students into an encounter with Christ in sacred scripture that I started seeing opportunities to use this process to teach about other things too. That same approach can be used to teach about the sacraments, the Creed, morality, prayer, or Catholic social teaching. Whatever the topic, applying the lectio divina process can make life so much easier for a religious educator.

In order to apply this method beyond the Bible to teach anything related to the faith, we will slightly rephrase the steps and Pope Benedict XVI's questions as follows:

1. Learn: What does this teaching mean?
2. Meditate: What is Christ saying to me?

3. Pray: What can I say to Christ in response?

4. Contemplate: What conversion of mind, heart, and life is Christ asking of me?

5. Act: How will I make my life a gift for others?

These are the five questions that we will invite our students to ask either directly or indirectly during a lesson. We won't give them the answers, but we will help them discover the answers for themselves. Think of each step as part of a five-point checklist to evaluate every lesson you prepare. Did your students ask each of these questions in some way during the lesson? Make sure that they do.

Most lessons and faith formation sessions focus on a lecture or textbook reading alone. This is the intellectual part of catechesis, step one. It is the explanation of ideas, presentation of doctrinal content, and the exploration of what we believe. The rest of the steps are more personal and directed toward the individual human heart. Asking these questions and responding in an appropriate way will draw students into a real encounter with Christ. They will learn about God, and they will learn how to be in relationship with God, which will lead (we hope and pray) to loving God.

The following chapters explore in detail the significance of each individual step and provide effective and creative teaching techniques to encourage students to focus on these questions and embark on a journey of encounter. For now, though, let's look briefly at each step and see how it should be integrated into every lesson you teach.

LEARN: WHAT DOES THIS TEACHING MEAN?

Notice how the Latin word *lectio* is the root word for the common teaching practice of "lecture"? "Lectio" means "reading." For our purposes, we will refer to the lectio step as "learning," which includes the listening, reading, or watching by which our students receive new information. This is the intellectual part of a lesson—helping our students understand the meaning of a Church teaching. To learn is to make connections between new ideas and things we already understand. As we hear someone speak, read what they have written, or watch what they have created, our minds are constantly at work. The mind is a connection-making machine. Each new stimulus we receive is encoded in the brain by connecting to what we already know.

As teachers, we can explain new ideas, even religious ideas, by relating them to concepts that our students already know and understand. The challenge is to find the best way to make connections for someone who seeks to understand something for the first time. Good explanations must be followed by good questions from the learner. The more the learner tests new ideas and connections for correct understanding through practice, the better he will grasp them.

This is why Jesus proclaimed the Good News of the kingdom of God in parables. People understood the settings for the stories and, therefore, made connections between those stories and what the kingdom is like.

A proper understanding of what we believe as a Church puts our students in the best position possible to encounter Christ in the steps that follow. Grasping the correct meaning can be like the lead domino for the rest of this process. Of course, it does not always happen this way. Sometimes in a journey of faith, a person has a meaningful and heartfelt encounter or conversion experience, which gives them the motivation to learn and understand more deeply what the Church teaches. Our hope, of course, is that when we have taught our students well and they have mastered an understanding of the doctrines we present, their experience in the next few steps will lead them to more meaningful encounters with Christ.

MEDITATE: WHAT IS CHRIST SAYING TO ME?

Relevance is the key to long-term impact in religious education. We want young people to see and experience how what they are learning can have a deeply personal effect on their lives today. Many of our youth are not leaving the Church because of disagreement with essential teachings; they are just *drifting away*. The Church stopped being relevant to them (if it ever was), and they looked for what they thought was more broadly spiritual instead. Some said in surveys that they just weren't being fed. All this amounts to one key mistake: we are not making what we teach relevant to those who learn from us.

The answer to making the faith matter to our students lies in meditation, which enables us to make connections between a mystery and our own lives. Again, the mind is a connection-making machine, and so, indeed, is the heart. When we meditate on a mystery—whether in reading scripture, praying the Rosary, celebrating a sacrament, or reflecting on a Church teaching—we connect what God says to what we need to hear. We seek to discern what God is saying to us because, indeed, he is speaking directly to us when we learn about a mystery of the faith.

Our call as educators is to help our students be open to hearing God's Word. We must cultivate an environment of listening and providing tools to hear God's Word in whatever we teach. It is through that encounter with the Word and the connections they make to their own lives that our students find relevance. Distractions in meditation can be their North Star. What are they worried and thinking about in this very moment? How can we help them make a connection between their concern and the new way of seeing the Lord in what we teach today? The more we help our students make those connections, the more they will embrace what we are teaching as important to remember and practice in their daily lives.

PRAY: WHAT CAN I SAY TO CHRIST IN RESPONSE?

In most religious education classes, prayer takes place before class begins or at the end of class before the students leave. These routine prayer times are important and valuable, but there is a danger of making prayer an activity entirely separate from learning. Prayer, in fact, is a vital form of learning the faith.

We have a well-known phrase in Catholic liturgical theology that reads in Latin, *Lex orandi, lex credendi*. It means, "The law of prayer is the law of belief." In other words, we pray what we believe.

Our prayer and our beliefs are united as one, not separate. Therefore, prayer experiences in class should also be united with learning, not something separate.

Instead of praying only at the beginning and end of class, make prayer an essential part of the learning process for every lesson. Teach your students how to respond to God in ways appropriate to what they have learned.

We have as a Church such a vast treasure trove of prayers, devotions, and liturgies that we can integrate into our lessons. These prayer experiences should build upon and express in words and actions the beliefs that we are teaching. Help your students give voice to the responses they feel called to make to their encounter with Christ in your class by drawing on the rich prayer tradition of the Church.

CONTEMPLATE: WHAT CONVERSION OF THE MIND, HEART, AND LIFE IS CHRIST ASKING OF ME?

In the previous three steps, we have tried to guide our students into a state of understanding in mind and heart of what the Lord is saying to them. In this final in-class step, we help our students recognize how their encounters with God call them to conversion. If the other steps focus on what is *said*, this step focuses on what is *not said*. "Contemplative prayer is silence, the 'symbol of the world to come' or 'silent love'" (*Catechism of the Catholic Church*, 2717).

Pope Benedict XVI describes the goal of contemplation not in terms of what is said but of what is seen: "Contemplation aims at creating within us a truly wise and discerning vision of reality, as God sees it, and at forming within us 'the mind of Christ'" (*VD*, 87). Likewise, the *Catechism* describes contemplation as "a gaze of faith, fixed on Jesus . . . His gaze purifies our heart; the light of the countenance of Jesus illumines the eyes of our heart and teaches us to see everything in the light of his truth and his compassion for all men" (*CCC*, 2715).

Put simply, contemplation is an experience of communion with Christ. We experience a conversion as we are transformed more and more into the image of God. In his book *New Seeds of Contemplation*, Thomas Merton describes this transformation as one from the "false self," which is dominated by selfishness and ego, to the "true self," which is being what God calls us to be—in union with him.

Here we get beyond just the intellectual understanding or emotional connection; we get to a transformation. We learn to see things differently. To be a Christian is to seek constant conversion, constant turning and transformation ever more into the image and likeness of God. In this step, we give students the opportunity to spend time with the Lord in deep prayer and discernment.

Putting it in simple terms, St. Teresa of Avila describes contemplative prayer as "nothing else than close sharing between friends; it means taking time frequently to be with him who we know loves us" (*CCC*, 2709). Are our students drawn into a closer friendship with Christ at the end of the lesson? Do they know that God loves them? Do they want to return to class in order to encounter him again? These are the questions we will attempt to answer with a resounding *yes* after implementing the strategies described in this book.

ACT: HOW WILL I MAKE MY LIFE A GIFT FOR OTHERS?

Think for a moment about the sacrament of Reconciliation. Even though we have experienced the mercy of Christ through the gift of absolution for our sins, our obligation is not complete. From there we go and do the penance assigned to us by the priest.

The word *penance* has an interesting history. The original word for conversion in the Bible is *metanoia*. At some point in our Church's history, the word *penance* was used in place of *metanoia*. St. John Paul II defined penance as "a conversion that passes from the heart to deeds and then to the Christian's whole life" (*Reconciliatio et Paenitentia*, 4). As educators, we don't give students a penance, but what if we challenged them to live in a new way after their encounter with Christ in the classroom?

Think of this final step as an ungraded, even optional homework assignment. Whether the students are given the opportunity to carry out these actions is left in the hands of the Lord. And whether they rise up to the challenge when given the opportunity will depend on the level at which they experienced a true transformation in their encounter with Christ.

MAKE DISCIPLES, NOT THEOLOGIANS

One of my mantras for religious education is to "make disciples, not theologians." I have to constantly remind myself of this goal to clarify my real mission as a religious educator. Jesus' parting words to the apostles were, "Go, therefore, and make disciples of all nations, baptizing them in the name of the Father, and of the Son, and of the holy Spirit, teaching them to observe all that I have commanded you" (Mt 28:19–20). He did not, however, command his apostles to go out and train experts.

The apostles themselves were not experts. They were common men from nonexpert backgrounds. They were set in opposition to the scribes and Pharisees, who were the experts of the time. The Pharisees knew the Law well, yet many were not living it. They understood in their minds what the Law and the prophets said, but they did not embrace it in their hearts.

I know a good many theologians who are also disciples. I don't want to suggest that someone can't be both. What I am saying is that training our students to be theologians is not our goal. Should they choose theology as a profession, wonderful! For now, though, whether they are in a parish religious education class or a Catholic school religion class, we will make disciples.

In Matthew 23, Jesus attributes a series of woes to the scribes and Pharisees. He also offers some advice to his disciples that we should listen to as well. He says, "Do not be called 'Rabbi.' You have but one teacher, and you are all brothers. . . . Do not be called 'Master'; you have but one master, the Messiah. The greatest among you must be your servant. Whoever exalts himself will be humbled; but whoever humbles himself will be exalted" (Mt 23:8, 10–12).

As you read this book, I hope you will experience a change in your understanding of your role as a religious educator. The focus and attention will shift away from you, your desire to impart information, and even your ability to teach, and rest instead on Christ and the ways in which your students—your brothers and sisters—are drawn more deeply into an encounter with him. Christ is the only master and teacher. Drawing on the steps outlined in this book, inspired by lectio divina, your lessons will become a gateway into a life of grace—a life of discipleship.

1 LEARN
What Does This Teaching Mean?

A teacher's primary responsibility is not to teach; it is to ensure that students learn. That may sound like the same thing, but in practice these two approaches are very different. Many educators lead with the mindset, "I teach; they listen and learn." The unfortunate truth is that learning doesn't happen that way, at least not effectively.

As I listen to many teachers talk about their work and think back to my own experience in education, I realize that the stress of teaching can blind us to how actively our students are learning. We often fall into the trap of thinking that if we teach something to our students, then it is their responsibility to learn and understand it. We feel that we have done our part in presenting the information and it is up to them to rise to the challenge.

The biggest mistake I made in my early days in education was to focus almost exclusively on what

I was doing rather than on how the students were learning. I concentrated on *my* lectures, *my* Power-Point presentations, *my* lessons, *my* explanations, *my*, *my*, *my*, etc. Not only was this an ineffective approach to education, it was an exhausting way to teach! I was the active one, doing all the hard work, while the students were passively coming along for the ride.

When I shifted my approach from active teaching to active learning, the students started remembering so much more. They were the ones doing the work, while I was there to coach and guide. I would introduce ideas quickly and efficiently, while the students set out on a journey of discovery. This is the experience you will have, too, if you apply what you read in this chapter to your own method of teaching.

If our students are unsure about something we have taught, then it is our responsibility—not theirs—to come up with a plan to help them learn it better. We do not stop until they have mastered the material, because once they understand what we want them to learn, they are ready for that all-important encounter with Jesus Christ.

THE MASTERY MENTALITY

What happens when a student does not understand a concept? What happens when they perform poorly on a test? The response we make as educators depends on whether we have a "move-on" or a "mastery" mentality.

Educators with a move-on mentality record grades and check performance on assignments but do not use performance to inform their teaching. They move on without much concern for mastery. They would rather present everything they are expected to, hoping students get it, than spend time focused on making sure students learn what they are supposed to learn.

Educators with a mastery mentality, on the other hand, monitor student progress and make changes to the way they teach based on that progress. They see performance on assessments as feedback, sometimes prompting them to change their approach and explain concepts in new ways. They care deeply about the students' progress and want them to grow.

The tools and tactics in this chapter can help you embrace the mastery mentality. But first, it is important to understand how humans learn. Once you know how the brain works, mastery is much easier to achieve.

HOW THE BRAIN WORKS

The brain is made up of a network of neurons. Each neuron is connected to other neurons. When we learn something new, we make a connection between that new idea and another idea that we already understand. Within the brain, this means we biologically connect two neurons.

As we master that new idea or skill, the connections between those two neurons are strengthened more and more. In fact, as we learn something new we make multiple connections to ideas we already understand, deepening our comprehension through the various connections running through an entire network of neurons.

Here is the most important thing to remember: every new idea you introduce needs to be attached to an idea your students already understand. Therefore, you must ask yourself: What connections am I helping my students make? What do they already know and understand, and how does this new idea fit into what they already know? The best approach to ensure that connections are being made is to use one of what I call the Seven Scaffolding Strategies.

THE SEVEN SCAFFOLDING STRATEGIES

Recognizing that knowledge is constructed along neurological paths, some educators have found the analogy of scaffolding to be helpful in teaching. Imagine, for a moment, the construction of a building. As each new level is added to the building, a scaffold is elevated next to it to help construct and support it. Once the building is completed and sturdy, the scaffolding can be removed. Likewise, using a scaffolding approach to teaching means providing support while students learn new ideas. When this support is no longer needed, it is removed as students show mastery on their own.

Every idea that you introduce to students for the first time needs to be connected to ideas they already understand. Think of these new ideas as pieces of a building not yet attached to the foundation that is already there. As the teacher, you can use a scaffold to help connect the new to the old. Once that new idea is attached, you can remove the scaffold because that information is linked within your students' long-term memory—or, if it is a skill you are teaching, the skill has become automatic.

Here are seven ways to use scaffolding to teach new ideas, each of which we will refer back to later in this chapter.

1. ADVANCE ORGANIZERS

Post an advance organizer on the board in the front of the room or on a sheet of paper on the students' desks. Think of an advance organizer like a map or a table of contents for your lesson. Some teachers write their lesson objectives or curriculum standards on the board as advance organizers. Others list the main topics for the lesson of the day. Still others will use visuals like mind maps for students to reference as a lesson progresses.

This simple practice enables students to make connections between every new piece of information you introduce and the advance organizer that you have provided for them. They can see where each new piece of information fits on the map. This way the information you present is always associated at least with the advance organizer, if nothing else, in their brains.

Let's imagine, for example, you are teaching a lesson about sin. The advance organizer that you write on the board can be as simple as this:

1. Sin
2. Original Sin
3. Mortal Sin
4. Venial Sin
5. Free from Sin

You can also frame these topics in the form of questions:

1. What is sin?
2. What is original sin?
3. What is necessary for a mortal sin?
4. What are venial sins?
5. How are we freed from sin?

You can check off each item as you progress through the lesson, and students will be learning new concepts knowing exactly where they are on your map. When you introduce Adam and Eve, for example, they know you are in the original sin section of the lesson.

2. OBJECTS AND VISUAL AIDS

As Catholics, we have so many choices of visual aids to link new ideas and information together.

Everyday objects as well as sacramentals can help your students make connections to new ideas. Display the chosen object prominently and refer to it frequently during your lesson to help students make connections between the object and the new ideas. Coming back to our example lesson on original sin, you might decide to bring in an apple with a bite taken out of it or a rubber snake (or both).

3. SONGS AND CHANTS

Songs and short chants are popular with younger students. Setting sentences and words to a familiar tune or easy-to-remember chant helps with memory recall. Again, once the new ideas are mastered, the songs are no longer needed. They are very helpful, however, early in the learning process.

When I teach the concept of sin to young people, I like to use the saying "sin separates, the Savior reunites." The alliteration in this simple phrase makes it easy to remember, and I repeat it frequently during the lesson. I also set this simple definition of sin as separation from God and others to the birthday tune: "Sin separates me from you. Sin separates me from you. Sin separates me from Jesus. Sin separates me from you."

4. HAND MOTIONS AND OTHER GESTURES

Another effective way to teach new ideas is to use hand motions and other gestures to help students remember the meaning of words. The students will rely on these gestures at first, and you may even see them mimicking them during tests, but eventually as new ideas are mastered, the gestures are no longer needed.

Gestures are very helpful in teaching definitions. Take mortal sin, for example. The three conditions for a mortal sin are (1) grave matter, (2) full knowledge, and (3) deliberate consent. Each condition itself is difficult to understand without further explanation. So, to assign a gesture to each one of these conditions, you can direct the students to (1) make a shocked face or a big frown to indicate the serious nature of the sin (grave matter), (2) point to the side of their head to show that a person must know what he is doing (full knowledge), and (3) point toward their heart to indicate that a person must freely choose to commit the act (deliberate consent). The students can even make all three gestures at the same time: shocked face, finger pointed to their heads with their right hand, and thumb toward their heart with their other hand.

Hand motions and other gestures work well in combination with songs and chants. Take my example of "sin separates, the Savior reunites." Students clasp their hands together, then separate them while they say "sin separates," then clap them together when they say "the Savior reunites."

5. GRAPHIC ORGANIZERS

Many people are visual learners rather than verbal learners. They understand ideas better when they are presented in images, charts, graphs, or other visually distinctive ways rather than strictly through words in line one after another. A graphic organizer is a handout that represents the connections between ideas in images rather than simply as words. Students remember how each idea is associated with other ideas depending on where it appears on the graphic organizer.

Using a graphic organizer is often the best way for students to absorb information as they listen to lectures or read a textbook. It allows them to more easily process what they are hearing or reading and make connections between ideas as they go. Graphic organizers can also be great tools for students to practice what they have learned, helping make new connections to ideas that have not been introduced in class but that they know from elsewhere.

To teach the difference between a mortal sin and a venial sin, for example, you can create a Venn diagram to show their similarities and differences. A Venn diagram is two circles that overlap with each circle labeled as one of the two connected ideas. So in our example, one circle is labeled Mortal Sin and the other Venial Sin. Ask your students to write the similarities between the two types of sin in the space created where the two circles overlap and the differences in the separate spaces of the two circles.

6. DEMONSTRATIONS

Demonstrations can be an effective way to scaffold a particular skill. You as teacher may perform the step-by-step process that you will subsequently ask your students to perform using a set of instructions. The demonstration models for the students the skill you want them to master. Sometimes you must do this demonstration multiple times in order for your students to grasp the process.

Think of this in the same way as watching YouTube videos to fix something around your house. You often have to view those videos multiple times before you can repeat the process you have observed in the demonstration. The more you watch, the more likely you are to execute the skill correctly.

During a lesson on sin, you would probably introduce the practice of an Examination of Conscience (a meditatio practice that we will come back to in the next chapter). Provide a list of questions to help your students make an Examination of Conscience, but you should also model for them what it is like to go through each question, drawing from your own life experiences as you reflect on each point. This will be an effective demonstration of the thought process you want your students to learn as they make an Examination of Conscience.

7. IDEAL EXAMPLES

Similar to a demonstration, an ideal example is simply a finished project or assignment that displays what you want students to create. Ideal examples set the standard. Showing nonexamples of lower-quality or unacceptable work can also set a standard of expectations for students before they begin.

At some point during your lesson, you will ask the students to complete a project to show what they have learned. Some students will do the least amount of work possible for this assignment. Therefore, setting a high standard ahead of time raises the quality of everyone's work.

For a lesson on sin, you might direct the students to create two different collages—one for mortal sin and another for venial sin. Since these are abstract concepts, giving the students examples of the kinds of images and words they can find in old magazines will be very helpful. This isn't giving them the answers but ideas about what to look for. It will also help them know the number of images and words they should include.

LECTIO LESSON PLANNING

We can now apply the Seven Scaffolding Strategies—advance organizers, objects and visual aids, songs and chants, hand motions and other gestures, graphic organizers, demonstrations, and ideal examples—to a lesson plan. Whether you are the kind of educator that plans out every minute of class or someone who lists a long agenda hoping to get through it all, this simple framework will help you organize your lesson plans:

1. Preparation
2. Presentation
3. Practice
4. Proof

(You can find more detailed lesson-plan templates at www.thereligionteacher.com/templates.)

PREPARATION

WRITING LESSON OBJECTIVES

Before you plan the activities students will do in class, make sure you have clearly defined your goals or lesson objectives. Ask yourself, "What do I want my students to be able to do at the end of this lesson?" Write out the answer to that question at the top of your lesson plan.

I recommend the common practice of starting each lesson objective with the words "Students will be able to," which you can shorten as SWBAT. Follow SWBAT with an active verb, then complete the sentence with the skill or idea you want the students to master. This way, your lesson objectives are not a list of activities for students but instead the desired outcome of those activities. In other words, your stated objective says exactly what you want your students to learn or master through the lesson. Here are some examples:

- Students will be able to (SWBAT) list the four gospels in order.

- SWBAT describe the key parts of Jesus' life as they are depicted in the gospels.

- SWBAT compare and contrast the synoptic gospels with the Gospel of John.

- SWBAT make connections between their lives and the life of Jesus.

I recommend setting at least one affective objective that focuses on the heart. Instead of writing "students will be able to," write an objective that "students will feel" (SWF) some emotion.

For example:

- Students will feel (SWF) excited to read more parables from the gospels.
- SWF happy for the people who experienced healing in the gospels.
- SWF guilty for the times they denied Jesus as Peter did during the Crucifixion.

PREPARING YOUR STUDENTS

The first five to ten minutes of class are the most important minutes you spend. Set the tone for a focused and effective class with the following simple strategies.

1. Bell Work

Have an assignment ready for students to work on as soon as they walk in the door. This is the single best way to engage your students because it immediately sets the tone for the day and reminds them of things they are learning in class.

Bell work can either review what the students learned in the previous lesson or preview some topics for the day. It can also provide opportunities for routine meditations such as preparing for the gospel reading at Sunday Mass.

Remember, learning is all about making connections. This assignment should help establish the connections you want to make in the lesson for the day. The more you jog the students' memory, the more you can build upon what they know with the new ideas you will introduce.

The assignments you provide as bell work must keep the kids actively engaged. The worksheets should make them think. Resist the temptation of assigning pages out of the textbook to read during this time because students will easily let their minds wander. The only exception is to assign pages while providing them with a graphic organizer to use as a reading guide.

Students finish bell work at different paces depending on when they arrive in class and how well they are able to complete the assignment. Have a few additional assignments on hand so that students who finish faster do not bother their neighbors who are still working.

2. Prayer

Gather together in prayer with a short and simple offering to God. Students will also be learning through prayer experiences later in the lesson (see chapter 3), but for now, set the tone for class as a prayerful environment where they can expect to encounter Christ.

3. Advance Organizers

Before heading out on a long road trip, most travelers consult a map to make sure they know where they are going. When someone sits down to read a new book, she is likely to review the table of contents first to see what the book explains and in what order. Likewise, it is a good idea to use an advance organizer to provide a structure for students to follow during your lesson. Refer back to this advance organizer throughout the lesson so the students know the context in which every new idea should be organized within their brains.

As mentioned earlier, an advance organizer can be as simple as an agenda of topics or a list of questions written on the board in the front of the room. You can also use the sections of your textbook as the outline of your lesson plan or create your own handout or graphic organizer to use as a guide.

4. The Hook

The temptation might be to jump right into the lesson now that you have outlined where you are going to take the students; however, there is still one more step to take to prepare your students for a great learning experience. It is called the hook.

The hook is the best way to begin constructing your scaffolding for a lesson. I first learned about this practice in Doug Lemov's book *Teach Like a Champion*. Through the hook, you tap into your students' prior knowledge so that you can build on it later during the lesson. The hook is something interactive and interesting. It is not explanatory. The purpose of the hook is not to teach new ideas but to establish a foundational set of concepts that you can make connections to later when you teach about the topic of the day. Here are some common ways to hook your students' attention before you begin the lesson:

Object: Imagine that you are to teach about baptism. Rather than beginning your lesson with an explanation of what baptism is and means to us as Catholics, spend just a few moments unlocking some prior knowledge to build upon during the lesson. The most obvious way to introduce a lesson on baptism is to bring in a visual aid: water.

With a cup or bowl of water on display at the front of the room, invite students to share what they know about water. This is how you begin to construct the scaffolding needed to build upon this knowledge later with a more thorough explanation of the meaning of baptism. You can begin by asking questions like "What do we do with water?" and "What would happen if we didn't have access to water?" Then, later, when you present new information about the sacrament of Baptism, refer back to the water and what students already know about it to connect the meaning of the sacrament to that prior knowledge.

Metaphor: You can also make a connection to something the students already know by using a simple verbal metaphor. In our baptism lesson, for example, use the metaphor of taking a bath or going for a swim to help build the foundation to teach about washing away our sins through baptism.

Story: Find a relevant story from scripture, the lives of the saints, current events, school or parish events, or your own personal testimony. The human brain is wired to remember stories, which makes them a great way to hook your students' attention. Share the story of your own baptism or, if you have kids, your child's baptism. Tell the story of Jesus' baptism or the baptism of a famous saint. It may take some research, but once you have the story, you can use it repeatedly throughout the year to remind your students of the meaning of baptism.

Song: To integrate music into your lessons, find a relevant praise and worship song to use in class or get a recording of a song commonly sung at Mass in your parish. When students hear the song later, they will be reminded of what they learned in class. You can also use popular songs in class, but make sure they are appropriate and that the meaning you try to attach is similar enough to the meaning the musician had in mind. For a lesson on baptism, songs such as "Morning Has Broken" or "Baptized in Water," both sung to the same tune, are appropriate.

Video: A lot of educators use videos in class these days. Remember, the purpose of the hook is not to teach new ideas; it is to tap into knowledge that students already have. Therefore, the videos you play for the hook should be inspirational stories or demonstrations of real-life events. Save the explainer videos for the presentation section of your lesson. Instead, show a video of someone's baptism to help students experience what they will learn about during the lesson.

OTHER WAYS TO PREPARE

There are many other ways to prepare students for a lesson. You may choose to focus on a scripture quote of the day or a saint of the day before beginning the lesson. These can be providential ways to make connections when you present new material in the lesson. Sometimes a feast day or the gospel reading of the week provides a good hook without your even planning it. The beginning of class can also be a good time to review homework and establish the prior knowledge that you will build on during your presentation and their practice time in class.

PRESENTATION

Speaking is not the only or even the best way to teach, but for some reason it has become the method teachers use most often to encourage learning in the classroom. Most of us had educational experiences that were primarily listening. It is an essential part of communication without a doubt, but the only way to ensure that students are learning is to make sure they are actively listening.

For students, active listening means constantly making connections to what they see and hear. It means doing something as they sit and listen to you talk. So when you plan your presentation, always keep in mind what your students will be doing as you talk. Following are a few points to consider as well as methods you can use to more effectively lecture.

THE AGE-TO-ATTENTION RATIO

With so much exposure to technology and social media, it seems that young people's attention spans are shrinking more and more. How long can they listen and pay attention to you speaking? Early on in my teaching career, I heard a rule of thumb that has proved to be true again and again. It is called the Age-to-Attention Ratio. Basically, it says that students can only pay attention for as many minutes as they are old in years. So, a second-grade student is likely to pay attention for 7–8 minutes at a time. An eighth grader has about a 13- or 14-minute attention span. Even a high school senior can only give you their attention for a little less than twenty minutes.

The obvious conclusion here is that you need to lecture a lot less in class. At some point as you are speaking, your students max out. They can't absorb any more new information. They need to shift to another activity, recharge their brains with a different form of learning, then prepare themselves to listen and learn again.

THE RULE OF THREE

Not only are students maxed out in the amount of time they can listen actively, but the human brain also maxes out when presented with too many new ideas at the same time. In general, students remember only three unique ideas at once. Even then, it helps to make sure those three ideas are united by one main idea.

You will be tempted, of course, to try to teach every term and concept in every chapter of the book. Here is the simple truth: the textbook contains more information than you can possibly cover in a year. What can you do? Forgive yourself. You can't teach it all. Let the overwhelming number of concepts go, and focus on just three at a time. The alternative is overloading the students so that they learn nothing.

When you read through the textbook for your next lesson, highlight just three new ideas to introduce to your students. When you plan your presentation, make sure to confine the lesson to no more than those three ideas at one time. You can go into detail about all three ideas, but at the end of the day, expect your students to recall information only about those three topics.

POWERPOINT PRESENTATION TIPS

A lot of teachers lecture with Microsoft PowerPoint (or Apple Keynote or Google Slides). This method allows you to add a visual element to the three main ideas you are teaching. You can add details and type words more quickly than you can write them on the board.

The mistake that many teachers (as well as conference speakers) make is to overload their slides with bullet points and text. It is impossible to listen and read at the same time. Listening and reading require the use of the verbal processing part of the brain, and we cannot process verbal information from two sources simultaneously. So instead of filling up the slides with text, save it for your lecture notes.

Use the slides as visual ways of connecting ideas. Offer images to support what you are saying. Include words that you are defining so your students can spell them and even read the definitions along with you. Just be careful not to put everything you want to say on the slides. Say it; don't slide it.

DON'T BE AFRAID TO DRAW

If you don't want to spend time creating a slide show and instead plan to use a whiteboard (chalkboard,

SMART Board, overhead projector, etc.), consider supplementing the text you write with drawings. Adding visual elements to your whiteboard lessons can be extremely effective for students. Remember, your lectures construct the scaffolding your students will use to connect new material with previous knowledge and recall the information later. The visuals you draw on the board can establish that scaffolding.

John Bergsma's drawings in his *Bible Basics* books are perfect examples. Dr. Bergsma was voted as a standout teacher at the Franciscan University of Steubenville for multiple years because of his unique lecture style. In college scripture courses, he uses stick-figure drawings to supplement his verbal teaching. The result? Students understand and remember what the stories in the Old Testament mean. Since it is easy to recall and even draw those stick figures, the students remember what the symbols and settings represent.

In one of your next lectures, draw a stick figure to help portray the main ideas you want to get across to the students. In the figure's hands or on its body, draw symbols to represent these ideas. Draw a setting around the figure to help get those ideas across.

Going back to our lesson on mortal and venial sin, for example, you can draw two stick figures.

Draw a coffin around or next to the figure representing mortal sin (grave matter). Place a light bulb above its head to show the second condition for mortal sin (knowledge that the action is wrong). Finally, add chains or handcuffs on the ground next to the figure (free choice to commit the sin). Draw the stick figure representing venial sin holding hands with Jesus or situated in a church. But turn this figure toward the mortal sin figure (because venial sin weakens our bond of charity with God) and taking steps toward that figure (since venial sins can sometimes predispose us to greater sins).

If you do not feel comfortable drawing stick figures with your lectures, make sure you represent the words in some visual way on the whiteboard. How are the ideas you are teaching connected? Are they meant to be compared? Is there one main idea followed by subsequent, more detailed ideas? How can you show the connections between the many ideas you teach? These questions should lead you to visually arrange the ideas on the whiteboard to show students how to make those connections in their brains too.

NOTE TAKING AND GRAPHIC ORGANIZERS

The single most important thing to think about as you plan your presentation is not what you will say;

it is what your students will do. How will your students follow along? What will they do while you speak?

The standard activity, of course, is taking notes. But let's pause for a moment and think about what that means. Do you want your students to write down everything you say? Are they just going to copy what you wrote on the board? This is, after all, the way many of us were taught to learn, right?

If your students take notes, make sure you lead them through an analysis of what they wrote down. Direct them to reread the notes and highlight, circle, or star the most important ideas you want to convey. This short, simple return to their notes can be incredibly effective in making connections within the brain. You cannot rely on your students' ability to do this on their own time. You have to lead them through the process yourself.

The alternative to a broad array of note-taking skills is to give your students a graphic organizer with guided notes to complete as you talk. This way, you highlight what is most important and arrange that information in a visual way for them. In other words, you visually make the connection between ideas for them so that when they are listening to you lecture, they know how the concepts you introduce fit into the graphic organizer and into the network of ideas already at work in their minds.

There are a lot of templates you can use for graphic organizers. You can find my collection at www.thereligionteacher.com/graphicorganizers. Search for some of the following templates online or create your own customized graphic organizers:

- Mind Map/Concept Map
- Venn Diagram
- Inverted Triangle
- Fishbone Map
- Spider Map
- Idea Rake
- Idea Wheel
- Sandwich Chart
- 2-Column Notes
- 3-Column Notes
- Problem-Solution Map
- KWL Chart
- Cause-and-Effect Chart
- Flow Chart
- Comparison Matrix

- Events Chain
- Sequence Chart
- Timeline
- Reading Strategies

It may be that you decide to introduce new ideas through reading rather than lecturing to the students. The same principles and tactics can be applied to reading from a textbook or primary source material. Limit the amount of time spent reading so that students are introduced to only a few ideas at once. Help them make connections with visuals and graphic organizers. Following are a few key ways to teach with reading.

PREREADING STRATEGIES

Think of prereading a section out of the textbook as an advance organizer for the students. Preview the images and ask students to make predictions about what the section is about. Do the same with headings and subheadings within a chapter. Focus on the headings, vocabulary words, and images and invite your students to make up questions before they start reading. Write those questions on the board as "What is . . . ," "Why did . . . ," or "How are . . . ," etc.

READING GRAPHIC ORGANIZER

Give students a handout to complete as they read. You can give them a list of questions to answer as they read, but a graphic organizer is even better. Again, a graphic organizer visually represents the relationships between ideas. So this requires you to read ahead of time what the students will read and find or create an appropriate graphic organizer that helps them to make connections between the most important ideas in the text.

Remember, you want to encourage active learning, which in this case means active reading. Otherwise, most students will let their minds wander as they read without context or purpose. If they have something to do while they read, they are much more likely to remember what they read.

AFTER READING

When students finish the reading assignment, the job is not done. The challenge now is helping them recall what they have learned so they can make connections between the new ideas they read about and what they already know—or to make connections between all the new ideas themselves. Sometimes the review questions in the book help students to think about and make these connections.

The next phase of your lesson should encourage students to strengthen the connections that have been made between ideas. Before moving to this phase, though, give your students a chance to reflect on what they read and help them summarize longer sections of the text. Ask them to write a sentence summarizing each section or to answer the questions they created in the prereading you did with them.

PRACTICE

The practice part of a lesson should always take up more time than the presentation. As human beings, we learn more by doing than by listening. The more time you give your students to apply what you have presented, the more likely they are to make those connections you want them to make.

Just as practice is essential for success in sports and the arts, it is vital for success in education, including religious education. A coach will spend a short amount of time drawing up plays on a whiteboard, but he knows the only way to make those plays a success is to practice them. He shows his team a play, then has them repeat it in practice again and again until they get it right. Likewise, the ballet dancer must practice her performance repeatedly rather than merely design a set of dance moves on paper and assume mastery.

In the practice part of your lesson, the first four steps in the lectio divina process take place: learning, meditation, prayer, and contemplation. Plan activities that challenge students to learn by making mental connections between ideas (lectio). Give them the opportunity for meditative practices to make connections between what they are learning and what is going on in their lives (meditatio). Establish a prayer practice to complement what they are learning so that the students can experience what they know in conversation with Christ (oratio). Give the students some time for silent prayer as well, in order to recognize their growing unity with Christ (contemplatio). All these activities are more effective than a simple lecture, and they should take up the majority of your class time.

We will come back to the ways in which you can guide your students through meditation, prayer, and contemplation practices in subsequent chapters. For now, consider these general suggestions for how to use your students' practice time to foster understanding of the ideas you seek to teach.

GRAPHIC ORGANIZERS, PART 2

I cannot emphasize enough that learning occurs by making connections between ideas. A graphic organizer, you will recall, displays the visual connections between words and ideas. Therefore, completing a blank or partially filled out graphic organizer will help students recall the connections between the ideas you presented.

Many of the worksheets in your students' textbooks can be considered graphic organizers. Likewise, you may find worksheets and handouts online that portray the connection between ideas. These are ideal worksheets for your students to complete during their practice.

Beware, however, of worksheets that do not challenge students to think. Many handouts available on the internet are simply busywork. Your students will be busy, but they may not be challenged to make connections. A word search, for example, does not encourage students to make connections between ideas. An exception might be a list of questions with the answer clues contained in a word search.

Mazes, coloring sheets, and similar activities can be fun for free time, but they are not something you should invite students to do as a way to learn. Class time is meant for learning to make connections both in the head and in the heart. There should be a direct link between the connections students are practicing and the presentation you just provided, so make sure the handouts you select connect with what you have taught.

Remember, your goal is to make disciples. You want to foster the opportunity for your students to have a meaningful encounter with Christ—a life-changing encounter with Christ. Will a word search challenge them to conversion? Will a pencil-drawn maze lead them to the kingdom of heaven? Will a coloring sheet help them see the Lord around them? These activities may be good entertainment, but they are not opportunities for encounter.

CENTERS/STATIONS

One of the most efficient ways to organize the practice part of your lesson is to distribute the activities you have planned at three or four stations around the room. Divide the students into groups, and give each group 10–20 minutes at each station before rotating to another station. As the educator, you can move around the room helping students when the other members of their group cannot help them first. Quickly scan their progress and spend more of your time with the students or assignments that require the most help.

You can also use these centers for recurring activities and games. Prepare a bag of supplies or handouts that do not require much explanation. When the students arrive at the center, they will immediately get to work rather than sit and wait for you to remind them of what to do.

Finally, centers offer the opportunity for parents to get involved in your classroom. Invite them to sign up to help out at centers throughout the year. They will enjoy seeing their children in the classroom setting and experiencing the lesson for themselves. They will also take a little more ownership over the lessons you are teaching. Plus, it frees you up to spend time on the stations with more difficult assignments.

PROJECTS

The practice part of your lesson is also a good time to spend on long-term projects. Projects, if carefully chosen, may push students to creatively make connections. And projects are the kind of assignment they keep and remember for a very long time. These activities are worth the sacrifice of class time if you believe in the process students go through to complete the assignment. Plus, spending time on projects in class relieves the burden parents sometimes feel in helping students with projects they don't completely understand.

If you assign a long-term project, give demonstrations and use ideal models to show students what to strive for. The more you demonstrate and set a high standard, the better projects you will get from them.

PROOF

The final part of your lesson isn't final at all. When you have proof that students can demonstrate your lesson objective, then you can move on. When the proof isn't there yet, you and your students still have work to do. The results from simple measurements you conduct in class will determine what to do next. If they understand, you can move on to add more ideas. If they didn't get it, you need to go back and re-present and practice more.

What we are talking about, of course, is assessment. The most common form of assessment is a quiz or test, but I encourage you to break away from that limited view. Our inclination is to see quizzes and tests as evaluation tools to help us give grades. We tend to see them as the end, not the beginning of some further instruction. Instead, find creative ways to check student understanding on an ongoing basis. This is called formative assessment—assessment that you use to form additional classroom instruction. Try some of the following alternatives to quizzes and tests.

Class Q&A: A class Q&A is probably the most common and quick type of formative assessment. Quiz the students at the end of class to see if they have learned what you wanted them to learn. Call it an end-of-the-class review. Turn your lesson objectives into questions and listen to the ways students answer. Be sure to call on a variety of students rather than just the few who you know learn quickly. If you did your job well, everyone in the class should provide some form of an acceptable answer. If not, it is your responsibility to go back and re-present and give the students more time to practice what they have learned.

Exit Cards: Distribute index cards for written responses to a question or prompt. Write the question on the board or state it out loud. Give the students 1–2 minutes to write their responses as best they can. The index card now becomes their exit ticket to give to you as they walk out the door. This format allows you to easily scan through their answers and check off the number of students who answered sufficiently.

Gist Sentence: You've heard the phrase, "I got the gist of it," right? It means that you understand the basic idea. You may not have all the details, but you grasp the important parts. A gist sentence is a statement of the main idea related to the lesson. Tell your students to write one sentence summarizing "the gist" of what you taught them. They can write this sentence on a piece of paper or even on an exit card for you to assess.

Newspaper Headline: If the students were to write a newspaper article summarizing the lesson, what would the headline be? What would the headline be for a blog entry or an online article? Direct the students to write that headline as a way to summarize what they learned. It is a creative activity that gives you the chance to see what they got out of a lesson.

Graphic Organizer: Yes, graphic organizers can be an effective form of assessment, too. Give students a blank or partially filled-in graphic organizer that summarizes the lesson and see what connections they can recall between ideas.

Self-Assessment: Sometimes it is best to let students evaluate their own mastery of a topic or skill. Ask them to give themselves a rating from 1 to 10 on how well they understand the lesson for the day.

You can also request that they tell you broadly what the main ideas of the lesson were. The more details you get during this self-assessment, the better you can determine how accurate their self-identified scores are.

Thumbs-Up, Thumbs-Down: Another quick way to gauge student understanding is to ask them to give you a thumbs-up if they understand and a thumbs-down if they don't quite get it yet. The more thumbs-up you get, the more you know you are on the right track in your lesson. Do this frequently during class so you know where to spend more time presenting or practicing. Just be careful not to rely only on self-assessment methods like this one because the students may think they understand something that they haven't fully mastered yet.

Using these and other tactics, you should now have some proof or at least strong evidence that the students have mastered the material at an appropriate level. If this is the case, then you can move on to the next set of ideas, which will build upon what you have already taught them. You will review, of course, and re-present ideas to help them understand new things you teach. Just remember, learning is a process, and it requires constant proof to know if your students are ready to continue.

DON'T STOP, THIS IS NOT BELIEVING

I urge you, please: do not stop here. The strategies in this chapter will help you teach about the doctrines and beliefs that we have as Christians. You now have an arsenal of tools to help students form understanding by making connections between ideas. These tools and tactics, however, are things any teacher of any subject can use.

In this first step of the lectio divina learning process, we seek to answer the question, "What does this teaching mean?" The goal is objective and intellectual, but you must not stop there. As a religious educator, you must get subjective and personal with what you teach. No matter how well your students have learned and understood what you have taught, it means absolutely nothing unless they personalize it. It is useless knowledge unless you invite your students to continue on to the next steps in the lectio divina learning process.

Now that they know what the Church believes, you can begin to help them personally believe these things, too, after an intimate encounter with Jesus Christ. From this education of the head, you will help them shift to the heart. You will help your students not only learn about the Lord; you will help them learn to love the Lord through meditation, prayer, and contemplation.

2 MEDITATE
What Is Christ Saying to Me?

When we narrow our focus to our most essential goal as religious educators, it comes down to this: we want our students to have a personal, lifelong relationship with Jesus Christ. As St. John Paul II wrote, "The definitive aim of catechesis is to put people not only in touch but in communion, in intimacy, with Jesus Christ" (*Catechesi Tradendae*, 5).

In order to meet this goal, therefore, you need to invite students to encounter Christ. You want them to personalize what the Church teaches and make it their own. You want them to know about Jesus so that they can begin to relate to him. How do your students relate to God? Through prayer and meditation.

From this point forward, you will look at the content of your lessons as opportunities for encounter. Your role is to go beyond ideas and definitions and statements of belief. Your job is to get students past learning about God toward learning to love God. You do this by making every belief you share with the students something that they will want to embrace in a personal way. You are seeking to make religious education relevant to their everyday lives.

FROM LECTIO TO MEDITATIO

In the last chapter, we looked closely at the most effective strategies and tactics for intellectual understanding. The goal is to encourage students to make mental connections between what they already know and the new things they are learning. From our perspective as religious educators, the goal of lectio is to build the foundation upon which students can enter into an encounter with Christ.

During the practice portion of your lesson plan, you will push your students to go further than just a simple understanding of the ideas. Using the strategies in this chapter, you will help your students recognize an opportunity to encounter the living Christ right in your classroom. Now that they have made connections with their minds, they will make connections between their minds and their hearts. "We pass from thoughts to reality" in meditation, says the *Catechism* (*CCC*, 2706). Students will listen in silence to the message God is speaking to them through whatever new belief they ponder.

Imagine you are teaching a lesson on the Eucharist. How do you get your students beyond learning alone and into a personal meditation on the Eucharist? You likely begin this lesson by introducing the students to Church doctrine on the Eucharist. You teach them terms like Real Presence, transubstantiation, Communion, Precious Blood, and Blessed Sacrament. You probably teach them about the Last Supper and the institution of the Eucharist. You might invite your students to learn about the parts of the Mass and the significance of the many prayers said by the priest and the faithful during the Eucharistic Prayer.

As an "encounter educator," however, you won't stop there. You know that teaching about transubstantiation is not enough. You need to help your students make connections between this mystery of faith and their personal lives. You need to help them meditate upon this mystery of faith so that they pass through that abstract idea to a personal reality.

PAST, PRESENT, AND FUTURE

The goal of meditation is to make connections between a mystery of faith and our own lives. This is how the mystery is opened up with deeper meaning. As we meditate on it, we make connections to our own experience, and those connections illuminate the meaning of the mystery for us.

There are three ways to make connections in meditation: past, present, and future. Let's imagine that you are teaching a lesson about the gifts of the Holy Spirit. Once you teach your students the proper understanding and definition of each gift in the lectio part of your lesson, you can help them make connections between the gifts and their memories of the past, concerns about the present, and hopes for the future.

Past: Guide your students to reflect on their memories, searching for moments in which they demonstrated one or more gifts of the Holy Spirit.

Present: Ask your students to think about what is going on in their lives right now. Which of the gifts do they need the most today? Which of the gifts do they have now and can use today?

Future: Invite your students to imagine their future at various intervals of time: tomorrow, a week from now, next year, as graduates, as adults, etc. Which of the gifts will they personally need the most in life?

The beauty of this approach is that each student has different memories and hopes for the future and, therefore, each student is drawn toward the gifts in unique ways. Here they can turn to the Holy Spirit to guide them toward a gift that they feel connected to the most.

Not to jump too far ahead, but the obvious next step in your lesson and in the lectio divina steps is oratio (prayer). In this lesson, you will invite the students in a creative way to ask for and accept the gifts of the Holy Spirit that attract them the most. Having had that prayer experience, they can look at their lives today and in the future with a new identity. They will see themselves as people with the gifts of the Holy Spirit who are able to overcome the challenges they meet in life.

START WITH STORIES

The simplest way to lead students in meditation is to invite them into an encounter with Christ through stories. For most of us, it is difficult to understand and remember abstract ideas but very easy to remember stories. We are built to connect with and remember stories.

When we read a novel or watch a movie, we make an emotional connection with the characters. They feel real to us. We become emotionally involved in their stories. Think objectively for a moment about how silly it is for us to shed tears during a sad (or happy) movie about people who do not exist. They are not real. Why do their stories make such an impact on us?

The reason is that we are wired to make emotional connections through stories. We relate to the characters. In the aftermath of an experience with a story, we may ask ourselves what it would be like to live out the lives of the characters in those stories. Kids do this naturally after watching movies. Think of all the young, imaginary Jedi knights you've seen in recent years due to the popularity of *Star Wars*.

The same experience can happen in your classes as you help students reflect on stories that relate most to the beliefs you are teaching them. Where can you find these stories? Following is a list of sources to search for relevant stories that will help your students enter into a meditation within your lessons.

Sacred Scripture: The purest and most natural source of meditation, of course, is sacred scripture. Through meditation on the stories in sacred scripture we go directly to the source: God himself. As part of your lesson on the Eucharist, for example, your students can read or hear the stories of the Last Supper, the road to Emmaus, or St. Paul's accounts of the Last Supper and Communion feasts.

The Lives of the Saints: There are so many saints in our Church's history! Many religion textbooks include relevant stories in each chapter. If students can imagine what it was like to live as that saint lived, then they can make the connection between the topic of the chapter and their lives today. You can also use saints' feast days to help make these connections. Many saints have been profoundly influenced by encountering the stories of other holy men and women throughout history, so including stories of the saints in class opens up the possibility of the Holy Spirit (perhaps with a particular saint's intercession) drawing your students into a deeper relationship with Christ. So many saints had a deep devotion to the Eucharist that the real challenge may be narrowing your focus. If it helps, pick a few of your favorite saints and search for their stories.

Your Life: Do not be afraid to share your own personal witness and testimony as it relates to the topic of the day. The story of how you came to believe what you teach is absolutely vital for your students to see how they can make that leap of faith as well. If they hear about your struggles in life and how a mystery of faith led you out of that hardship, they can relate that story to their own struggles. When they hear your stories of God's gifts of joy and gratitude, they can look for opportunities to experience those graces as well.

For example, tell a story about a memorable Mass. Tell them your earliest memories of going to church. Tell them what you were thinking at the most recent celebration of the Eucharist (even if you were distracted). These personal stories are a gateway for the students to experience the Eucharist in similar ways and begin to make their own memories and stories to share with others.

Contemporary Servants: Consider telling stories of modern-day servants of God, such as the pope or bishops or fellow teachers and ministers. Their stories can also help your students make connections between what they are learning and their personal lives.

How does the pope encounter Christ in the Eucharist today? Can you find stories or videos of him celebrating Mass or praying before the Blessed Sacrament in eucharistic adoration? What about famous Catholics or your local leaders? What do they personally like most about the celebration of the Mass? Share these stories if you can.

Remember, these stories are only the starting point. A good story alone does not guarantee that your students will meditate on the mysteries of our faith. You have to encourage them to make connections between the story and their lives. The strategies that follow will help you do that.

VISUALIZATION AND GUIDED MEDITATIONS

Guided meditations are an effective way to make the mysteries of faith personal to your students. If you start with a story, guide your students to use their senses to enter more deeply into the story. Our senses (seeing, hearing, feeling, smelling, and tasting) make things real. They have a potency when attached to memories. Helping students activate their senses during meditation makes things more personal and real for them. I encourage you to try the following forms of visualization with your students. Both actively engage the senses.

The Observer: One form of visualization is to imagine yourself as an observer in the story. Help your students imagine being physically present but not involved. What do they see in the scene? What do they hear? What do they smell? What does the setting feel like? A good novelist helps her readers relate their senses to a scene in her story. In the same way, help your students add details to their visualization as an observer.

The Participant: A second form of visualization is to imagine becoming one of the people in a story. Encourage your students not only to enter the story through their senses but also to feel the emotions of the person in the story they are relating to. The more they connect with the specific experience of that person, the more real it will become for them, and the more likely they are to make connections to their own lives either at that moment or later, when they have a similar experience.

Back to our lesson on the Eucharist. You have introduced the main ideas related to our beliefs as Catholics about the Blessed Sacrament. Now use these two forms of visualization to help your students enter into a meditation on the Last Supper or the Mass.

In our first example, you would read the story of the Last Supper to the students and then guide them to imagine themselves being there as an observer. What do they see? What are Jesus and his disciples wearing? What does the room look like? What do they hear Jesus saying? What do the disciples say that may not even be in the biblical text? What do the bread and wine (and maybe even candles or oil lamps) smell like?

Now invite your students to imagine participating in the Last Supper as one of the disciples. Beyond that first set of meditation questions, help them think about how they feel in reaction to Jesus' words. Repeat the words for the students, pausing between each of Jesus' statements. What emotions do these words evoke for them personally? What do they want to say to Jesus in response?

You can also guide students through a meditation on the Mass. Direct them to imagine themselves sitting at Mass. Help them enter into this meditation by evoking their senses. What and who do they see in the church? What do they hear and smell? What does the pew feel like? What do the Body and Blood of Christ taste like?

Then help your students get beyond the senses and into their emotions at Mass. Knowing what they know about the Eucharist from your lesson, now they can make connections to their lives and add meaning to these beliefs. If your lesson focuses on Eucharist's meaning of "thanksgiving," for example, what do your students feel thankful for? Help them make connections to those feelings of gratitude. If your lesson focuses on forgiveness of sin and unity with Christ, guide your students to think of specific sins and guilt that are keeping them away from opening their hearts and minds to Christ. For what do they want forgiveness? How do they feel knowing that at that moment of receiving Communion, they are forgiven for their smaller sins and brought into deeper union with God?

Do not forget that the visualization itself is not the goal of meditation. The goal is for your students to make connections to their own lives through that visualization. You want them to connect that experience to their personal lives.

When guiding your students through a meditation on a story, remember to utilize past, present, and future. When have they had similar experiences in the past? What thoughts or emotions are they experiencing right now that are similar to those of the people in the story? When can they expect to encounter a similar scenario in their lives? How will they react? Helping bridge the gap between the stories and their lives will prompt them to ask the key question you want them to answer in these meditation strategies: *What is God saying to me?*

A CONVERSATION WITH CHRIST

The act of meditation does not have to be kept completely separate from the act of prayer. Another popular form of visualization is to guide students to picture themselves having a conversation with Christ. Having learned something new or having heard a story about a mystery of faith, they can now talk with Christ about it. Invite them to let the Holy Spirit inspire within them words that Jesus himself might say to them. They can imagine themselves saying something back, having a true conversation, and seeing what comes out of that encounter.

For example, instead of just imagining the Last Supper, invite your students to speak up during the meal. What do they ask Jesus? What does he say in response? What do the other disciples say? Letting these conversations play out in their heads can be a beneficial way to discern what God is saying to them through this lesson.

Likewise, encourage your students to visualize a conversation with Christ after Communion. Having received his Body and Blood, what do they say to Jesus? What does Jesus say back? Frame this conversation in the context of what you taught them. Following are a few ways to organize this kind of imaginative meditation.

Quiet Meditation: Direct the students to close their eyes and use their mind's eye to imagine themselves sitting side by side with Jesus and having a conversation. They can talk within their heads, saying nothing out loud and writing nothing down. Ask rhetorical questions to guide the students through this conversation.

Journal: You can also direct students to think through their conversation with Christ by having them record what they might hear and say in a journal. They can write down something Jesus would say and then write their response, like a script for a play or a movie.

Conversation Starters: Some of your students may struggle with this form of meditation at first. They may not be able to get in the right frame of mind to visualize this conversation. To help them out, create a worksheet with the beginnings of sentences that Christ or they might say during the conversation. This will give the students a head start in coming up with something to say to Christ. The extra benefit is that these starters will guide the conversation directly to what the students are learning during this particular lesson.

Whatever format you use, just make sure this conversation is serious and meaningful. Truly, this imaginative form of prayer can be the lived experience of an encounter with Christ within the context of what you are teaching.

MEDITATION AND MYSTAGOGY

Another way of looking at meditation is to think of the Church's practice of mystagogy during the RCIA. After going through the catechumenate and receiving the sacraments, the newly baptized Christians are led through a period of meditation on their experience of the Sacraments of Initiation. This is called "mystagogy" because it is during this time that they come to more fully understand the mystery of the encounter they experienced.

The sacraments are an essential part of being Catholic. We experience them throughout our lives, and they often come and go so quickly that we do not take the time to meditate on their specific meaning for us. That is why mystagogy is a valuable form of continuing catechesis even in the classroom.

Are there sacraments that directly relate in some way to the topic you are teaching right now? Help students remember their experience of those sacraments. If they cannot recall their baptism or reception of another sacrament, review with them each step or symbol within the rite. Help them visualize experiencing these things once again, using the methods described in the previous section.

Then, take that next most important step: mystagogy. Help your students connect the experience to their lives. Help them make the experience of the sacraments real, personal, and meaningful.

In a similar way, you can help students unpack the experience of a mystery of faith. You are passing on a truth of faith that helps us understand more intimately who Jesus is. Unpacking this mystery objectively can lead to an understanding of the mystery subjectively. Guided meditations will help your students grasp the meaning of the truth to them personally through their past, their present, or their future just as newly baptized Christians experience mystagogy.

MEDITATING ON WORDS AND PHRASES

Focusing on one word or phrase is a popular form of scriptural lectio divina. Rather than examining an entire passage, invite your students to choose a quote or even one word and focus attention on it and nothing else in the reading. With the help of the Holy Spirit, memories and thoughts may surface as they relate to that word or phrase.

This method can be applied beyond scripture to the mysteries of the faith. If you are teaching multiple terms and topics, guide your students to focus on only one word or phrase that they are learning and try to relate their personal lives to that one idea. Students can also pick a word or phrase in a definition or description of these topics you are teaching them.

For example, in a lesson on the Eucharist, students might meditate on one of the many terms associated with the Eucharist: Real Presence, transubstantiation, consecration, host, Blessed Sacrament, Body and Blood, New Covenant, Last Supper, Mass, etc. Tell them to write this word at the center of a blank sheet of paper and then jot down around it thoughts or memories as they occur. Your students can reflect on the ways this word connects to their memories or what they are thinking about in their lives right now. In that way they can start to discern what God is telling them through this topic.

Students can also focus on a specific definition. For example, you might invite them to reflect on the definition of transubstantiation as the changing of the bread and wine into the Body and Blood of Christ during the consecration at Mass. Supply questions for their meditation or let them write down random thoughts and memories that come to them.

Afterward, they can make connections to the definition to see what might be relevant to them right now. Your meditation questions might be something such as:

- What else changes in its form?

- How have I changed into someone or something different in my life?

- How can I receive the Eucharist with more reverence knowing that Christ is truly present in the bread and wine?

ICONS AND IMAGES

Iconography is a popular source of meditation in Eastern churches. Icons help Christians enter into a meditation on the scene or saint they depict. Looking at a holy image for a prolonged period, observing details, and then letting memories and thoughts surface can be a good way to meditate.

Consider taking your students on a field trip to your church to see the stained-glass windows or other images and statues there. Focus on just one image. Explain to your students what the image is meant to show (lectio), then help them find personal meaning in connection to the image (meditatio). Bring with you a set of meditation questions to help them make connections between what they see and what is going on in their lives right now.

The added benefit of these meditations in church is that the students will attach memories to these images that stick with them for a very long time. They might, in fact, always see these images as a personal reminder of something God wants to tell them. This can transform the church into a home for your students. They will associate memories with this place and its artistic images and begin to see there the presence of God.

INDUCTIVE EXAMINATION

So far, the meditation methods we have described start with a Church teaching and then lead students to relate their personal lives to that teaching. This is what the *National Directory for Catechesis* calls the deductive method of catechesis. The deductive method begins "with the general principles or truths of faith and [applies] them to the concrete experiences of those to whom the catechesis is addressed" (*NDC*, 97). Using the deductive method in a lesson on the Eucharist, for example, you help students think of life experiences that relate to the theological teachings about the Eucharist they learned.

Another approach is the inductive method of catechesis. "The inductive approach proceeds from sensible, visible, tangible experiences of the person, and leads, with the help of the Holy Spirit, to more general conclusions and principles" (*NDC*, 97). In this approach, you invite students to recall their memories and pressing concerns, then relate those personal experiences to the lesson of the day.

The most popular methods of recalling our life experiences in order to discern what God is calling us to be and do are the various forms of Examination of Conscience. Many people are familiar, of course, with the examination recommended in preparation for confession in the sacrament of Reconciliation. These guided meditations include lists of questions usually based on the Ten Commandments to help us discern the sins we have committed. This can be a very effective form of examination when done in the context of a specific series of lessons. Instead of the Ten Commandments, for example, create your own Examination of Conscience specifically related to the lesson you are teaching.

Another form of examination made popular by St. Ignatius of Loyola is the daily examen. This is an act of meditating on one's day. With the guidance of the Holy Spirit, you can help your students remember each important (and seemingly unimportant) moment of their day. Help them find moments to be grateful for and offer them up in thanksgiving to God. Encourage them also to look for moments in which they felt God's presence—moments that may not have been obvious until they took the time to reflect.

Examining their day can be a very effective starting point for your students to discern what the Lord is saying to them today. You can also use these examinations to connect to the introduction of new ideas and new truths of faith. Drawing on their daily memories identified during the examen exercise, you can guide your students toward new ways of recognizing how to see God and how God sees them.

GROUP DISCUSSION AND REFLECTION

Have you ever been a part of a Bible study or Bible-sharing group? The purpose of these groups is to join together to read and discuss a passage from the Bible or a spiritual book. The group members are not there to teach one another. There may be a group leader who helps clarify and explain the reading, but the purpose of the group is to gather and share personal connections to what was read. The group gathers to share what the text says to them, not just what it says objectively. These kinds of Bible groups are opportunities for meditation.

You can set a similar goal with the group discussions in your class. Divide your students into groups to share personal connections they are making to what they are learning. As the students hear their peers share stories, they can better relate and connect to the aspects of the faith they are learning about in class. The more students share their personal stories, the more others in the group are inspired to also share. The following are a few best practices when gathering for group discussion.

Use Discussion/Reflection Questions: Give the students questions to reflect on and answer together as a group. Clarify some of the questions for them if you do not hear a lot of talking.

Go from Personal to Public: Make sure that the students answer the discussion questions on their own before joining in the group. Once they have come up with answers to the questions, they have no excuses for not sharing in the group. Plus, you can check for participation with the written answers or a completed graphic organizer.

Model Good Discussion: It may help early in the year to model good discussion practices for the students. Show them how to share and how to respond to someone else's story in an appropriate way. Demonstrate this with some volunteer students in the front of the class.

Enlist Group Leaders: Parent volunteers can help guide discussions so that everyone shares and everyone makes those personal connections they should make during meditation. Let your volunteers know that some silent thinking time between sharing is expected, but encourage them to ask questions to spark additional discussion and even share their own stories to help students make their own personal connections.

Do a Class Review: Once the class comes back together, take some time to unpack and review what students talked about in groups. This will help them clarify what God is saying to them and what they might be called to change in their lives because of the discussion.

THE WORDS TO SAY

As Christians, we can find it difficult to discern what God is saying to us purely by listening. We are also invited into a conversation, a communion with Jesus Christ. We listen (something we may not do enough these days), but we also speak to God. Meditation can become an isolating act unless it leads into a connection with Christ.

It is necessary to guide your students through the difficult task of discernment—to think and imagine and feel—but you can't stop there. You must also encourage them to respond. That response will help them remember that they are cultivating a relationship with Christ, not just learning interesting ideas. In a relationship, people listen and speak. Now that they have heard what Christ is saying to them in meditation, what will they say in response through prayer? Thankfully, the Church has two thousand years of words to help with this response, and it is your job to teach these words to your students.

3 **PRAY**
What Can I Say to Christ in Response?

I love that every time I say "thank you" at the fast-food restaurant Chick-fil-A, I hear the employees answer, "My pleasure." It is subtle, but the more you hear it, the more it stands out. Clearly, the team has been trained to say these two words, which are a departure from the more popular "You're welcome." My guess is that it puts a smile on the faces of other guests like me who say thanks after ordering food. Without a doubt, the employees take true pleasure in the smiles on people's faces, too, and all they needed to do was follow the directions given in their training.

In a lot of ways, our rich history of Catholic devotions and liturgical prayer is like this. The Church's prayers provide for us the words to appropriately respond to an encounter with Christ. They give us words when we may not know the right thing to say. These words must please God, and they give us the satisfaction of responding to God in the best way we can. In the case of religious education, these words help students pray what they are learning to believe. The words of our prayers act as scaffolding for the construction of a language we can use to talk to God. They teach us what to believe without us even realizing it.

LEX ORANDI, LEX CREDENDI

The approach to prayer in this chapter is different from the way many religious educators approach class prayer. All too often, prayer becomes something to check off the list of to-do items for the day. Certainly prayer should be implemented to begin and end each class, but we have to be careful not to make prayer something separate from the learning experience. When we teach our students to pray, we also teach them to believe.

Lex orandi, lex credendi means "the law of prayer is the law of belief." Believing and praying are not separate acts; they are intimately linked. In fact, prayer leads to belief. The more we pray in a certain way, the more we believe fully in the words that are said.

This is why as Catholics we practice so often the ancient forms of liturgical prayer and memorized devotions. With all our liturgies, litanies, novenas, and other forms of prayer, we have words to say to the Lord that can lead us to believe and love him in new ways.

Prayer is therefore an essential way for students to learn during a lesson. Lead your students through prayer experiences that help them pray what they are learning. Whether or not you take the time to explain and unpack the words that they say, the important thing is to give them words to pray and actions to do that relate directly to what you want them to learn to believe.

MEMORIZED PRAYER

So how do you make rote prayer something students personally embrace and integrate into their daily lives? Try some of these approaches:

Set the Tone: What kind of prayer is it? What mood should your students be in when reciting the prayer? Think of visuals to use in the room to accompany the prayer. Or play some music before (and possibly during) the prayer to help get the students in the right frame of mind. Dim the lights or go outside, depending on the kind of prayer you want to use.

Meditation Comes First: Don't forget that before prayer comes meditation. The memorized prayer you teach and pray together should come after the students have made meaningful and personal connections to the Catholic teaching they are learning. Then, when they pray to support and further understand this teaching, the prayer is built upon the foundation of those personal connections. This way, the words they pray become reminders of the connections they have made. It is a way of personalizing traditional prayers even if they are just read or recited from memory.

Repeat: Our rich devotional life as a Church is built upon the habitual repetition of certain prayers. They are most effective when repeated day after day. The students may not think they get anything out of reciting the prayers at first, but over time those repetitive phrases sink into their subconscious. They will start to notice moments throughout their days that connect with the prayers. They will start to live what they pray, but only once those phrases are engrained in their minds can they seep into their hearts.

Pre-/Post-Prayer Discussion: Introduce prayers with a quick survey of the words you will use and how they connect with the lesson of the day. This will help your students make mental connections while they pray. Do the same after the prayer is completed. Go back through the words and ask students to point out connections with what they learned (lectio) or how their life experiences relate (meditatio).

PRAYERS AND DEVOTIONS TO USE IN CLASS

Let's review what you are trying to accomplish with prayer in your lesson. Your first goal is to help your students grasp the meaning of certain ideas and mysteries of the faith (lectio). Next, you invite your students to make personal connections between these teachings and their lives. Out of those connections, you guide your students to come to recognize what God might be saying to them, calling them to change in some way (meditatio).

That realization, that discernment, is solidified through the response they make to God in prayer. You can either invite your students to make up their own prayers in response to their meditation or provide for them the ancient, tried-and-true prayers of the Catholic Church. What follows are just a few examples of the many Catholic prayers and devotions you can use to help students pray to God in response to their encounter with him. The key is to add personal meaning to what can become the monotony of memorized prayers and devotions.

THE LORD'S PRAYER

This, of course, is the way Jesus taught us to pray. The early Christian Tertullian called the Lord's Prayer "truly the summary of the whole gospel" (*CCC*, 2761). In the words of the prayer we find God's identity as Father, Son, and Holy Spirit, and we are given models for petitioning God. We pray in union as a Church and with God's Son to the Father, who is in our heavenly home. Then we recite seven petitions, which, as St. Thomas Aquinas pointed out, "not only teaches us to ask for things, but also in what order we should ask for them" (*CCC*, 2763). In other words, the Lord's Prayer teaches us how to pray.

On the one hand, you can pray the Lord's Prayer with your students on a routine basis to begin class or end class. For the purposes of this chapter and this lectio divina approach to lesson planning, however, you can also use the Lord's Prayer as an important part of the learning experience. There are so many opportunities to connect the words of the prayer to the lessons you teach. The key is to highlight the words that have the most relevance and pray with that connection in mind.

For example, in a Catholic social teaching lesson on the theme of Option for the Poor and Vulnerable, your students may meditate on the times they have encountered people in poverty. They may come to recognize the ways God is calling them to serve the poor. The phrase "give us this day our daily bread" takes on new meaning when prayed in the context of this lesson. So also does the "our" in "Our Father," as your students recognize more fully that God is the God of all people, both rich and poor.

Each part of the Lord's Prayer, in fact, can be related to the Church's teaching on poverty, making the praying of it a heartfelt experience of solidarity with the poor and vulnerable. You can focus on the comparison between the richness of heaven and the injustice of earth. You can highlight the temptation to ignore the poor or the evils that cause poverty. After a reflection on the prayer helping students make these connections, pray it together, uniting your minds and hearts with the heart of the prayer. This can transform your students' perspective on the prayer, but it can also transform the students themselves, leading them to a mini-conversion.

THE HAIL MARY

It's no surprise that the *Ave Maria*, the Hail Mary, is the second most popular prayer among Catholics. Not only does it venerate the Blessed Virgin Mary as the Mother of God, but it attests to one of the most important things for us to remember about the

Church: we support each other. We turn to the Virgin Mary to ask for her intercession. She prays for us. Likewise, we can turn to the saints and ask for their intercession, just as we can turn to a friend and fellow brother or sister in Christ to pray for us (the saints, however, are especially close to Christ).

The Hail Mary is a short prayer, but it can be meaningful when associated with the students' meditation on the mystery of faith you are teaching. Help them make connections between the prayer and what they are learning, then pray it together during your lesson as a way to internalize the mystery through prayer.

Think of ways you can make connections between the Hail Mary and a lesson on a theme from Catholic social teaching. Guide your students to reflect on these questions: Who can I ask Mary to pray for? In what ways have I sinned by accepting an injustice in the world without compassion or action? The Hail Mary can be a perfect way to respond to the Church's social teaching on life and death issues. When we pray "now and at the hour of our death," we can also pray for those who die due to injustice: abortion, the death penalty, war, etc.

THE CREED

When you invite your students to pray the Creed (either Apostles' or Nicene), think of it as a bold statement of belief, not a list of teachings. In other words, the Creed gives us the words to state our belief in God. Encourage your students to say the words with their hearts, not just their heads—to say thenm and mean them. It is very likely that some part of the Creed has particular relevance to what you are teaching on any given day. Highlight that part of the prayer. Help your students to thoroughly understand what it is they stake a claim in believing when they say the words. The more depth and meaning you add to each of the phrases, the more the students can take ownership over their faith.

In reciting the Creed, we state, for example, that God the Father is the "Creator of heaven and earth," "of all things seen and unseen." These words have a profound impact in reference to a particular theme of Catholic social teaching, care for God's creation. If your students truly believe that God is the Creator, then they must see themselves as stewards of that creation. He created the world good. They should keep it that way. If you have effectively explained the meaning of this theme and invited your students to meditate on its implications for their lives, then you can help them see the deeper meaning that comes from calling God the Creator of heaven and earth in the Creed.

THE LITURGY OF THE HOURS

The Liturgy of the Hours, otherwise known as the Divine Office, is the Church's official daily cycle of prayer. Bishops, priests, deacons, and religious are required to pray the Divine Office every day. The prayers, psalms, hymns, and readings within each of the hours are filled with wisdom. They are beautiful and poetic. They give us a wealth of expressions to communicate with God.

Reciting the hours, even just one of them, on a daily basis can be very fruitful. The words sink into your mind and heart. The Spirit may remind you of them throughout the day to apply what you have prayed in specific situations. That is why you might find some value in leading students regularly in Morning Prayer, Daytime Prayer, or Evening Prayer depending on the time of day that you teach.

You can also expose students to this form of prayer sporadically throughout the year, especially when you have a relevant lesson to connect to it. You might invite your parish priest or deacon to class to introduce the students to the Divine Office.

Just as you did with the Lord's Prayer, Hail Mary, and Creed, help students understand the meaning of the words they pray before they pray them. Point out the particular connections between each part of the prayer and the lesson of the day. In a lesson on the Catholic social teaching theme of Solidarity or Rights and Responsibilities, for example, focus on connecting the hymns and psalms of the Liturgy of the Hours to the definition of the theme. In reciting the Divine Office in a community, two groups alternate between verses. When the students recite the Office in this way, explain that this is a physical expression of solidarity and of their responsibility to serve one another and the rest of the world.

THE ROSARY

Technically, the Rosary is meant for meditation. During each decade of the Rosary, the students should meditate on a mystery of the life of Christ and Mary. Help them make connections between each mystery and their personal lives. You can facilitate this meditation through pre-prayer activities such as journaling or other suggestions from chapter 2. You can also introduce students to the Rosary as a way to communicate with God. They can pray a Rosary for a specific purpose or with a special intention in mind.

Again, let's look at a social justice example. In a lesson on the encyclical *Evangelium Vitae* (*The Gospel of Life*) and the tragedy of abortion, students can pray a Rosary specifically for the men and women experiencing unexpected pregnancies or for the lives lost through abortion. Guide them to meditate on the Joyful Mysteries of the Rosary. This combination of prayer and meditation on the mysteries of Christ's birth and childhood can lead to a personal encounter with God's mercy.

OTHER CATHOLIC DEVOTIONS

There are many different devotions and prayers to introduce to students in the heart of each lesson. Remember, your goal is to find a prayer that fits well in your lesson. Choose devotions that enable students to meaningfully respond to their meditation on what God is saying to them. Once they have personalized what they have learned through meditation, they can now personalize the prayers they say in response. Consider introducing your students to these Catholic devotions sometime this year:

The Angelus and Regina Caeli: Church bells ring at 6:00 a.m., noon, and 6:00 p.m. each day to call Catholics to pray the Angelus (or the Regina Caeli during the Easter season). The Angelus can help your students redirect their minds and hearts to the Incarnation of Christ. By reciting this prayer, they recognize

God's presence among them no matter when and where they pray. They do so with a special devotion to Mary. Likewise, in the Regina Caeli they pray in union with Mary to give praise and thanksgiving for the Resurrection.

Divine Mercy: Originating with a revelation of Jesus to St. Faustina, this prayer has become a very popular devotion thanks to the influence of St. John Paul II. Introduce students to the Chaplet of Divine Mercy, which takes less time to pray than the Rosary, and the Divine Mercy image.

Novenas: There are many novenas that you can invite students and their families to pray. Send students home with a novena to pray together with their parents. The more closely these novenas are linked to what students are learning, the more they will be special ways to encounter Christ in the context of each lesson.

Stations of the Cross: Making the way of the Cross, especially during Lent, can be a powerful way to encounter Christ. The act itself is a meditation on Christ's Passion and Death. The words your students say at each station, "We adore you, O Christ, and we praise you, because by your holy Cross you have redeemed the world," can be an appropriate response to anything they feel God is calling them to be or do.

SPONTANEOUS PRAYER

As you read in chapter 2, spontaneous prayer while visualizing a conversation with Christ can be a great way to cultivate encounters with God. That conversation should be linked to the meditation you do in class. Such conversational style of prayer is critically important to help students realize that their relationship with God is personal.

The following are a few creative ways, other than visualization, for students to articulate a response to their meditation on the teachings they have learned.

Diary: Many young people start their diary entries like a letter, with the words "Dear Diary." In a similar way, your students can journal by recounting their days beginning each entry with "Dear Jesus." The intimacy of prayer should be similar to the intimacy with which someone writes in a diary.

Letter to God: Provide your students with a sheet of paper to write a letter to God. You can prepare this activity during their meditation with a letter from Christ to them. Their letter, then, is a letter written in response. You are inviting your students to write to answer this chapter's prayer question, "What can I say to Christ in response?"

Text Message: Recognizing that young people seldom write letters today, you can get creative about this conversation with Christ. Direct your students to write their prayers in the form of a text message. This may be short, but it can be fun as long as the kids stay focused on the mystery you want to open up for them. Offer some text message prompts from God to get them started.

Social Media: What if your students could communicate with God on the most popular social networking website or app of the day? What would they say in response to their encounter with him during the lesson? Challenge them to think creatively about how to talk to God about what they have learned and meditated upon in this lesson using social media. If you do experiment with this kind of creative prayer, make sure the students treat the activity with reverence.

THE FIVE FORMS OF PRAYER

The *Catechism of the Catholic Church* describes three "expressions of prayer" and five "forms of prayer." The expressions of prayer should look familiar because they match up nicely with three phases of lectio divina: vocal prayer (oratio), meditation (meditatio), and contemplative prayer (contemplatio). As the *Catechism* says, these expressions of prayer have one thing in common: "composure of the heart" (*CCC*, 2699). The goal of prayer is to connect with Christ in our hearts. Meditation, as you read in chapter 2, makes this possible through visualization and personal reflection. Through contemplation, which you will read about in chapter 4, we recognize our unity with Christ and the transformation he is calling us to make. What about prayer? How can we make sure that vocal prayer is also an act of the heart? That is where the five forms of prayer come in.

The five forms of prayer direct spontaneous prayer in appropriate ways. When designing the prayer-learning experiences for your lessons, keep each of these forms of prayer in mind and choose the form that fits best with the Church doctrine you are teaching. Following are brief summaries of each form of prayer with suggestions for how to design prayer experiences that enable students to understand more deeply the Catholic Church's teachings on social justice.

1. BLESSING AND ADORATION

Think of all the ways people use the term "blessing." People say a blessing upon food before meals. Children seek the blessing of their parents before making important decisions. Likewise, people turn to the Father and ask for his blessing upon them. When someone says he feels blessed, he acknowledges God's presence. He feels as though he has some special gift or ability without tangible proof. A blessing from God, therefore, is the recognition of the gift of his presence.

Many people may not be aware of this, but a blessing goes two ways. God blesses us, but we bless him back. "The prayer of blessing is man's response to God's gifts: because God blesses us, the human heart can in return bless the One who is the source of every blessing" (*CCC*, 2625). A blessing is "an encounter between God and man" (*CCC*, 2626). This is why blessing and adoration are linked together. To adore God is to recognize his presence among us and to acknowledge our role as creatures before the Creator. We stand before God in humility because he has blessed us with his presence.

In the classroom, help your students get in a position of adoration and blessing before God. Are they aware of God's presence? Do they recognize their position in comparison to the great almighty God?

To encourage your students to bless and adore God in a lesson on Catholic social teaching, for example, focus on teaching them about the dignity of the human person. Your students can ask for a blessing upon themselves and each other. They can ask for a blessing upon specific groups of people whose dignity is denied by society today. Then, they can bless God by reciting together the Divine Praises:

Blessed be God.
Blessed be His Holy Name.
Blessed be Jesus Christ,
true God and true Man.
Blessed be the Name of Jesus.
Blessed be His Most Sacred Heart.
Blessed be His Most Precious Blood.
Blessed be Jesus in the Most Holy
Sacrament of the Altar.
Blessed be the Holy Spirit, the Paraclete.
Blessed be the great Mother of God,
Mary most Holy.
Blessed be her Holy and Immaculate
Conception.
Blessed be her Glorious Assumption.
Blessed be the name of Mary,

Virgin and Mother.
Blessed be St. Joseph, her most chaste
spouse.
Blessed be God in His Angels and in
His Saints. Amen.

2. PETITION

This is the form of prayer with which your students
will be most familiar. To bring a petition before the
Lord is to ask him for something in a spirit of reliance upon him. Asking for forgiveness is a common
petition. Asking for help and healing are also common petitions to bring before the Lord.

In a lesson on social justice, guide your students
to meditate on the ways in which they have contributed to some injustice in the world. Then, during
this prayer of petition, invite them to ask for God's
forgiveness, seeking his mercy for the times they
have not shown mercy.

3. INTERCESSION

A prayer of intercession is a form of petition. We
ask for something from God on behalf of others.
We intercede on the behalf of others, and likewise,
we ask others to intercede to God on our behalf. As
Christians, we pray for one another. We pray for all

people, even our enemies and those we do not know well.

After sharing a lesson on one or more topics related to Catholic social teaching in which you describe the plight of a specific group of people, encourage the students to design their own prayers of petition for these people. Help them understand the pains these people experience. Help them put themselves in the shoes of these individuals so that they can offer an appropriate prayer of intercession before the Lord. Offer these petitions using the familiar format from the Universal Prayer (Prayer of the Faithful) at Mass, and you will make that Sunday experience even more meaningful for them.

4. THANKSGIVING

Expressing our gratitude to God is also a common way to pray. In fact, it has become quite popular in our culture to suggest a gratitude practice as a form of meditation whether done in the context of prayer or not. As Catholics, we express our gratitude directly to God, of course. Everything we have is a gift from God, and we express that to him in prayer.

During a lesson on social justice, your students may realize how much they have compared to the many who are lacking in food, work, or opportunity.

Encourage them to give thanks to God. This may evoke feelings of guilt for having so much when many people have so little—an important learning experience that can lead them to conversion. Or, if your focus in such a lesson is on social action, students can pray in thanksgiving for the progress their society has made in extending protection and justice to those who have struggled to get it.

5. PRAISE

Finally, to praise God is to give God all the glory and to tell him why he is so great in our eyes. We can praise God for the gifts he has given us, but we also can praise him simply for being himself. God is good, and we tell him so by citing all the examples of his goodness we have witnessed or heard.

When your students praise God within a lesson on Catholic social teaching, they express in words how wonderful he is for his mercy and justice. If every human person has dignity, then this is something to praise our Creator for giving us. Jesus came to "bring glad tidings to the poor" and to "proclaim liberty to captives" (Lk 4:18). These are reasons for your students to give God glory and praise.

PLANNING PRAYER SERVICES

Prayer services are closer to liturgical prayer than to regular prayer time in class. Prayer services include multiple forms of prayer and involve multiple people. The goal is to provide a memorable and reverent experience around a certain topic.

A prayer service is meant to be heartfelt. For that to be the case, plan for the students to participate in a prayer service after they have personalized the lesson's topic through meditation. Through meditation, they will gain some understanding of what God is saying to them personally today. Then, in the prayer service, they can make the words of the prayers their own words as well. They can offer words as a response to God after encountering him in some way.

Even better, however, is to integrate prayer and meditation in the same prayer service. With guided questions or reflection prompts, invite students to listen for God's word in their minds and hearts. Then, using the words written on the prayer aides, students can respond to God in an appropriate way.

Here is a basic format for prayer services based loosely on the Liturgy of the Word that you can use in class or in larger groups of students and educators:

1. Sign of the Cross
2. Opening Prayer
3. Scripture Reading
4. Meditation/Reflection Questions/Homily
5. Prayers of Petition
6. Contemplative Prayer Experience
7. Closing Prayer
8. Sign of the Cross

A couple of notes about this approach:

Opening/Closing Prayers: You can compose these yourself or find traditional prayers to adapt and use in class. Popular prayers such as the Prayer of St. Francis or St. Ignatius's prayer for generosity work well at the opening and closing of the service. The key is to make sure the prayers align with the focus of the lesson and the prayer service.

Contemplative Prayer Experience: We will come back to contemplation in the next chapter. In addition to a guided meditation and petitions tailored to the lesson, the prayer service can include a meaningful opportunity for deep prayer. This may mean silent reflection on something from the reading. It can be silent time before the Eucharist. It can be silent prayer before a holy image or icon. Nothing needs to be said or done other than to focus on the Lord and allow the students to meet him in some unique way.

PRAYER TABLES

Many religious education classrooms have prayer tables set up as reminders that God is present in the room. Make creative use of the prayer table to foster a unique prayer experience within each lesson you teach.

Bring in a lesson-specific symbol as the centerpiece of your prayer table. You can even use this symbol as the hook for your lesson, giving students some scaffolding to help them understand what they will learn. The symbol can also be used at prayer time to inspire the words to pray to God within the lesson.

For example, for a lesson on Catholic social teaching, invite your students to bring in canned food items and place them on the prayer table. Help the students visualize the individuals and families who will put these food items to good use, then pray for those people. The effectiveness of your lesson and the meditation will set the tone for this prayer time. The students will know what to pray for after a meditation on the Church's teachings about poverty.

Below are some other ways to optimize your prayer table for personally efficacious prayer time.

The Bible: Open the Bible on the prayer table to a passage related to the lesson of the day. Read and guide the students through a meditation on the passage, then invite them to pray in response to what they have heard.

Sacramentals: Many prayer tables have statues of Mary, a cross, rosaries, or other sacred objects on display. Use these sacramentals as the focal point of the lesson. Focus on them for a brief meditation related to the lesson of the day, then use them to inspire the appropriate words to pray in response.

Personal Items: Give students ownership over the prayer table by inviting them to bring in personal items to place on the table to inspire prayer. They can bring items in for specific lessons and use them during prayer time.

Prayer Box: Place a box or basket on the prayer table to hold intentions that the class will pray for together. Set aside special times during each class or on a weekly basis for students to add their intentions to the box.

Seasonal Items: Decorate the prayer table for the liturgical seasons. Adorn it with colors to match the season and bring in objects such as an Advent wreath or a crown of thorns that represent the focus of the season. You can refer back to these items frequently to remind your students of the spirit of the season.

FROM SAY TO SEE

The strategies outlined in this book so far will help your students learn about what the Church says, what God is saying to them, and what they can say to God in response. That is a lot of talking! Sometimes, though, we encounter Christ without words. It can be just as important to *see* God as it is to *say* something to God. Contemplation, which is the focus of the next chapter, helps your students move from something to say to something to see. After an encounter with Christ, your students will start to see the world and themselves in a different way. This is the ultimate goal of religious education, right? Remember the words of St. John Paul II: "The definitive aim of catechesis is to put people not only in touch but in communion, in intimacy, with Jesus

Christ" (*CT*, 5). This is also the hope and goal of contemplation.

CONTEMPLATE

What Conversion of Mind, Heart, and Life Is Christ Asking of Me?

In this book we have looked at the most effective ways to learn new ideas (lectio). We have provided a variety of ways to help students integrate those ideas into their personal lives (meditatio) and respond to God appropriately (oratio). To suggest that this next step can be achieved through simple methods and practices alone would be misleading. Contemplatio is different from everything we have discussed thus far.

Contemplation is less about what we do and more about recognizing who we are. There are very few methods to describe contemplation adequately. Instead, it goes beyond methods toward a new way of seeing. The learning strategies in this book build a mental foundation upon which your students can meditate and pray with their hearts. This prepares students to experience contemplation, which is the recognition of a transformation. In contemplation your students come to see how they have become united with Christ.

Thomas Merton's writings on contemplation and contemplative prayer are extremely helpful. He described contemplative prayer as "prayer of the heart." He wrote: "We do not reason about dogmas of faith, or 'the mysteries.' We seek rather to gain a direct existential grasp, a personal experience of the deepest truths of life and faith, finding ourselves in God's truth" (*Contemplative Prayer*, 67). This should sound pretty familiar since it is exactly why you are applying this process of lectio divina to your lessons. You want your students to experience an encounter with Christ and get beyond a purely intellectual understanding of who Christ is.

Contemplation sounds more complex than it has to be. St. Teresa of Avila described contemplative prayer as "nothing else than a close sharing between friends; it means taking time frequently to be alone with him who we know loves us" (*CCC*, 2709). To guide students to contemplate Christ is to give them the time to spend with him without any goals in mind. By recognizing his presence with them, they can see themselves in relationship with him. As a result, they will be in the best possible position to discern what God is calling them to be.

Meditation and prayer help your students personally experience those deepest truths of life and faith, but this final step, contemplation, helps them find themselves in God's truth. To find themselves "in God" is to find themselves in communion with him. To be in communion with him, they must recognize how he has transformed them and conformed them to his image.

METANOIA

What is the biggest reason that so many young people enrolled in religious education programs drift away from the Church, at least for a time? They learn a lot about the Catholic faith in school and parish education programs. They take classes for years. But they drift away because they have yet to experience an encounter with Christ that leads them to conversion.

You don't hear the Greek term *metanoia* among Christians anymore. *Metanoia* means literally "changing one's mind" (*meta* means "after" and *nous* means "mind"). It is the Greek word for conversion, but *metanoia* is translated as "repent," "repentance," and "penance" in the New Testament. People tend to think of penance as the act of seeking forgiveness from God. When someone commits a sin, they feel bad about it and turn to God for his mercy. Or within the actual sacrament of Reconciliation, penance is understood as an act to make up for a sin.

The modern-day misunderstanding of "penance" is far removed from the original meaning of metanoia, which is conversion. Penance is not a payment to God for obtaining his forgiveness. It is not a punishment to be served before forgiveness is complete. That is not the point at all. Instead, as we will see in the next chapter, penance should be an act that flows out of a conversion of the heart.

What does this have to do with contemplation in your Catholic classroom? Everything you have done up to this point has one goal: to help your students experience a conversion of the mind, heart, and life through an encounter with Christ. Your aim is to help them see God and their lives in a new way. They will repent, not just seeking forgiveness for doing wrong things but committing to live their lives in a new way.

Christianity is a religion of the Cross and the Resurrection. Jesus said to his disciples, "If anyone wishes to come after me, he must deny himself and take up his cross daily and follow me" (Lk 9:23). For your students to repent, they must let some part of themselves die. It is more than choosing to be a good person. Through your lesson, your students will choose to lose something they are attached to in order to follow Jesus more closely. They will make this choice knowing that God is with them, strengthening them in their ability to carry their crosses.

The first time repentance (metanoia) appears in the New Testament, it comes as a message from John the Baptist. He "appeared in the desert proclaiming a baptism of repentance for the forgiveness of sins" (Mk 1:4). In baptism we submerge in water as one person but emerge from the water as someone else. We die to our old selves and rise with Christ. We are free from sin and able to find union with Jesus Christ. The more your students understand this truth about their baptism, the closer they will grow to Christ.

CONTRITION AND CONTEMPLATION

It would be idealistic and unrealistic to expect your students to experience a life-changing conversion during every one of your lessons. Sometimes that encounter with Christ in class will make a lasting difference, a lasting change in their lives. At other times, they may recognize how they want to change but fail to do it. There will be many times, however, when your students just won't accept the fact that God is calling them to change in some specific way.

The Catholic concept of contrition can help. "Contrition," like "penance" and "repentance," is a word used to refer to conversion. Within the sacrament of Reconciliation, we make an Act of Contrition that goes something like this:

> My God,
> I am sorry for my sins with all my heart.
> In choosing to do wrong
> and failing to do good,
> I have sinned against you
> whom I should love above all things.
> I firmly intend, with your help,
> to do penance,
> to sin no more,
> and to avoid whatever leads me to sin.
> Our Savior Jesus Christ
> suffered and died for us.
> In his name, my God, have mercy.

Contrite people feel guilt and remorse for committing a sin. In addition, they have the intention of never committing that sin again. Sometimes through meditation and prayer, your students will recognize their sins. At other times, they won't feel guilt but instead a desire or resolve to change. They may feel called to do things differently or to stop doing things in some areas of their lives. These commitments align nicely with the experience of contrition.

There are two kinds of contrition. *Perfect contrition*, which is inspired by the love of God, motivates us to seek forgiveness and make the decision to change. *Imperfect contrition*, on the other hand, is often motivated by fear of punishment. Your students, for example, may decide to change something in their lives as a result of a reflection or planned activity in the classroom. That's good, but contrition is still imperfect if it is not motivated by the love of God. This is nevertheless a great starting point. We are planting seeds that may take a long time to grow.

Your goal is not to fill your students with guilt by the end of a lesson but to get them as close as possible to perfect contrition. You want the love of God to inspire them to want to make changes and give up whatever it is God is calling them to change.

Following are some specific activities you can do in class to help your students make the commitment to conversion.

CONTEMPLATION OF THE COMMANDMENTS

As we have done in the last few chapters, we will use an example lesson to talk through this step of lectio divina lesson planning. In this chapter, we will look at cultivating contemplation in a lesson on the Ten Commandments. Imagine what a lesson like this might look like up to this point.

First, you help your students understand what God and the Church say about the Ten Commandments. Using the Seven Scaffolding Strategies for the commandments as a whole or each one of the commandments, you help the students make connections with things they already know and understand. For example, you might make connections between the commandments and class rules or between the commandments and the Bill of Rights. You do the same thing for each one of the commandments, using scaffolding techniques to help students understand them individually. You spend only a short amount of time lecturing and more time guiding your students to practice and apply what they have learned so they can strengthen this understanding.

During the practice part of the lesson, you build upon your students' understanding of what God and the Church say about the commandments by

leading them into a meditation on what God is saying to them right now. You help them make connections between the commandments and their
memories of the past, their concerns about the present, and their hopes for the future. In this way, the
commandments become personalized and appli-
cable in their lives today. An examination of conscience is the perfect tool for a meditation on the
commandments.

Out of that meditation and recognition of how
the Ten Commandments are relevant to their lives,
you invite your students to respond in prayer. You
may invite them to visualize a spontaneous conversation with Christ about the commandments or help
them personalize the prayers of our Church. You
may introduce to them the Act of Contrition in such
a way that they fully understand the words they say,
especially after their meditation on the commandments. You may also introduce the students to the
Penitential Rite at Mass, the response at Mass before
Communion, the Divine Mercy Chaplet, the Miser-
ere, the Jesus Prayer, or even the Hail Mary or the
Lord's Prayer.

Finally, you come to contemplation. How can
you lead your students in contemplation at this point
in the lesson? You can either lead them through an
experience of deep prayer or you can guide them in

prayerful, contemplative discernment techniques that will help them recognize how God is calling them to conversion.

CONTEMPLATION AS DEEP PRAYER

Remember, contemplation is less about what we do and more about who we are in relationship with Christ. We can become so attached to methods of meditation and contemplative prayer that they become obstacles to communion with God. Many spiritual guides warn that the human heart may seek the solace of the methods more than a direct relationship with Christ. So look at the suggestions that follow as ways to get students to contemplate Christ's presence but not as ends in themselves.

Contemplation does not require listening or talking. While meditation is about making connections between a mystery of faith and our lives, contemplation may not involve thinking or emotions at all. In prayer, we speak out loud or in our minds, saying something to God in response to an encounter with him. The default form of contemplation, on the other hand, is silence. We simply spend time with God. We seek to be in his unspoken presence. To do this, we have to quiet our minds. The only goal is Christ himself.

Your students may not get anything out of contemplative prayer. Unlike meditation, in which they think about themselves and God, in contemplation you ask them to think only about God. Doing so helps them break away from their selfishness and start to see themselves as God sees them.

While you may not integrate the following practices into your class on a frequent basis, each of them can be a wonderful opportunity for your students to experience a contemplative encounter with Christ. As the *Catechism* says, contemplative prayer can be "the pre-eminently intense time of prayer" (*CCC*, 2714). That does not mean it has to be difficult or something only spiritual masters can achieve. Remember once again St. Teresa of Avila's description of contemplative prayer as "nothing else than a close sharing between friends; it means taking time frequently to be alone with him who we know loves us" (*CCC*, 2709). I hope you frequently offer your students the following experiences as times to be alone with Jesus.

SILENCE

Silence is so rare in our young students' lives. People young and old are constantly surrounded by noise and distraction. TVs stay on at all times in the home, and headphones seem to never leave the ears of young people today. They desperately need opportunities to get away from all the noise.

Think of contemplative silence not as the practice of absence but instead the focus on presence. In silent contemplation your students remove all distractions, leaving only the Lord. They recognize even in the quiet emptiness that God is present among them no matter where they are. Being aware of his presence and just sitting silently with him will fill them with hope and love.

How can you cultivate silence for your students? Build it into class time and prayer time. Give them the chance to sit silently in prayer. Instruct them not to focus on thinking or acting or doing. Let them just sit in patient, silent recognition that the Lord is present. Sometimes their thoughts will be a guide to discovering the Lord. That's OK. Encourage them to pursue the distractions, but always thinking of them in reference to what God wants to say through those thoughts.

EUCHARISTIC ADORATION

For many Catholics, myself included, the Eucharist and specifically eucharistic adoration played a significant role in their conversion or reconversion to the Catholic faith. Is it any surprise? Here is the physical embodiment of our God! Christ is truly present among us. Through eucharistic adoration we can physically spend time with our Lord. Adoration truly is the perfect form of contemplation.

Many schools and parishes provide times for exposition of the Blessed Sacrament. What suggestions can you offer your students attending adoration?

Model Mental Prayer: Let go of the obligation to monitor the students' behavior and focus your attention on Christ. Let the students see you so they know how to act. Show rather than tell them what is expected. Allow yourself to sincerely pray before the Blessed Sacrament in a way that shows students what mental prayer looks like. Focus on Christ and nothing else. We hope the students will start to do the same. If they don't, then spend time afterward explaining to them how they should act. They will have the memory of your example to recall and emulate next time.

Invite Them to Embrace the Silence: Tell them that they can certainly talk to Christ in their minds, but it is also beneficial just to sit and focus entirely on the Blessed Sacrament. Kids do not get much opportunity for silence, and sitting there before the Lord truly sanctifies the silence. They can use adoration time to do meditation and vocal prayer (to themselves), but silence is a unique opportunity.

Encourage Them to Do Meditatio and Oratio: If silence is too difficult for your students, give them some questions for meditation on a scripture passage. Allow them to bring a journal to write down their thoughts, emotions, and prayers in response to this meditation. Or invite them to practice a devotional prayer such as the Rosary or a Chaplet of Divine Mercy before the Blessed Sacrament. The Jesus Prayer can also help them focus their attention on Christ during adoration.

THE JESUS PRAYER

The Jesus Prayer is a simple, twelve-word prayer: "Lord Jesus Christ, Son of God, have mercy on me, a sinner." It is particularly important to Orthodox Christians and Eastern Catholics. The prayer is repeated continually as a mantra to clear the mind and focus entirely on Christ and our state in relationship to him. Thomas Merton, who expressed in his writings the need to let go of methods in contemplative prayer, conceded that the Jesus Prayer may be the one exception. Indeed, it is described by Eastern Christians as the method for achieving prayer of the heart.

The Jesus Prayer can be said during eucharistic adoration, or it can be integrated into classroom prayer experiences. Discuss the meaning of each part of the prayer or remind the students what the words say about Christ and us. Model and lead your students in reciting the prayer with long gaps in between each recitation.

PRAYING WITH ICONS

Praying with icons is another form of unspoken, intense prayer from the Eastern churches. In meditation, we make connections between our lives and what we see in a particular icon (see pages 84–85). We can also pray with an icon of Christ, using the icon as a focal point for vocal prayer. Even better, though, is the use of icons for contemplative prayer.

Remember that contemplation is a form of prayer that helps us see God and ourselves in a new way, unlike meditation and vocal prayer, in which we listen and speak with Christ. Icons can help us see God in new ways. They were created (the technical term is to "write" an icon) in a prayerful way intended for prayerful use.

The most popular form of icon is the *Pantocrator*, which is an icon of Christ. Using the wonders of technology, you can find a number of variations of the Pantocrator on the internet to pray with in class. You can prompt the prayer time with some guided meditation and prayer, but make sure you challenge the students to spend time in contemplation just looking at the image and clearing their minds of all thoughts and other distractions. The hope is that they grow closer to Christ during this time, not that they necessarily walk away with something to think or do differently.

VENERATION OF THE CROSS

We take time to venerate the Cross as the source of both sorrow and hope, especially during the season of Lent. In a contemplative act of veneration, we remember what Christ did for us as we gaze on a cross or a crucifix with Christ's body. Just sitting in recognition of Christ's sacrifice can lead students into prayerful gratitude for the gift of his life he gave to them. While Christ may not be physically present in a cross or crucifix, these sacramentals are powerful reminders of God's presence as the risen Lord.

Bring your class prayer table to the front of the room and place a cross or crucifix at its center. Invite the students to silently sit before this cross in recognition of the sacrifice of Jesus. If necessary, give the students meditation questions or prayers to recite silently. Otherwise, just invite them to sit with the presence of the Lord in mind.

CONTEMPLATIVE SONG

One way to foster contemplation through music is to repeat a simple prayer much like the Jesus Prayer in song. The continuous repetition of a single phrase accompanied by heartfelt music can focus our minds and hearts on Christ. This practice has become popular in praise-and-worship experiences in which a musician or band repeats one line of a song over and over. The repetition helps create in the heart a feeling of closeness to Christ.

Taizé prayer has become synonymous with this form of prayer. Parishes sometimes host Taizé prayer services that focus on simple phrases from the psalms or the liturgy sung reverently and repetitively. This form of prayer was inspired by the Taizé Community, which was founded in the mid-twentieth century as an ecumenical group of individuals dedicated to common prayer.

Using a CD, music from the internet, a guest musician, or yourself as a model, invite your students to prayerfully and repeatedly sing one phrase that connects with the lesson of the day.

CONTEMPLATION AS DISCERNMENT

What do the conversion stories in the New Testament have in common? Think of the call of the first disciples. They were fishermen. Jesus asks them to leave their nets and become fishers of men (Mt 4:19). Later Jesus meets Matthew, a tax collector, and calls him to leave there and come follow him (Mt 9:9). Paul, who persecuted and killed Christians, experiences a complete conversion, leaving his status as a respected Pharisee to spread the Good News of Jesus Christ throughout the Mediterranean.

Each of these stories aligns with Jesus' description of discipleship: "If any one comes to me without hating his father and mother, wife and children, brothers and sisters, and even his own life, he cannot be my disciple. Whoever does not carry his own cross and come after me cannot be my disciple" (Lk 14:26–27). Elsewhere Jesus says: "Whoever wishes to come after me must deny himself, take up his cross, and follow me. For whoever wishes to save his life will lose it, but whoever loses his life for my sake will find it" (Mt 16:24–25). Therefore, the purpose of each of the following activities is to help students discern what it takes to be a disciple. They will have to recognize what God is calling them to lose.

Remember that each of these activities and writing and reflection prompts is meant to follow a meditation and prayer experience. The students should already have an idea about what God is saying to them and what they want to say to God in response. Now they look inward to discover what this means about the person they are meant to become.

CONVERSION T-CHARTS

To make a T-Chart, draw a line down the center of a sheet of paper and label the two columns at the top of the page, making a T shape. The differences between the two columns show the conversion that the students can see in themselves.

OLD ME, NEW ME T-CHART

Jesus said, "Behold, I make all things new" (Rv 21:5). This passage comes from the end of the book of Revelation in which a new heaven and a new earth are taking form. The entire universe experiences a conversion. Things are made new. Likewise, when we experience conversion, we become a new person in Christ. We are formed into his image.

On the left side of the T-Chart direct your students to write "Old Me," and on the right side, "New Me." Tell them to describe the changes they feel God is calling them to make in their lives. This is a quick way for students to reflect on changes occurring within themselves because of an encounter with Christ through meditation and prayer.

The beauty of this activity is that it helps your students visualize their future. By putting down in writing what kind of person they know they should be, they are more likely to make the changes needed. The act of putting it in writing strengthens the commitment to follow through and take action.

Let's say that during your lesson on the Ten Commandments, the students meditated on the fourth commandment, making connections between "honor your father and your mother" and the way they have been treating their parents lately. After identifying the specific ways they have not honored their parents and responding to God in a prayer of contrition, they can experience contemplation. What kind of person is God calling them to be? The "old them" talked back to their parents, but the "new them" is respectful to their parents instead. In the left column they can write the specific ways they have not honored their parents, and in the right column they can write the ways they will honor their parents with God's help.

LOST AND FOUND T-CHART

Another way to think about conversion is a transition from lost to found. When we are lost, we are separated from God. We try to go about our lives on our own. Then Christ finds us and calls us to follow him. Where will he lead us?

On the left side of their chart ("Lost"), direct the students to write down the ways they were lost. What were they doing in life that was getting them nowhere? On the right side of their chart ("Found"), they can write how Christ found and loves them anyway. What does God's love feel like to them? What do they feel compelled to do for God in return?

This T-Chart works well in the contemplation of the first commandment: "You shall have no other gods before me." With your guidance in meditation, students identify the things they have elevated, even worshipped, before God. In their prayer, they ask for God's forgiveness and mercy. Through one of the forms of deep prayer discussed earlier, they can come to recognize God's mercy.

Now that they have experienced that mercy in deep prayer, they can identify what this experience means for them. Before their encounters with Christ, they suffered loss from the emptiness of putting things before God. They can write how they suffered under the "Lost" column. Under the "Found" column, they can identify what it feels like to experience God's mercy. They can also write what happens to them when they let God lead them instead of following something or someone else.

BLIND AND SEE T-CHART

Pope Benedict XVI wrote that contemplation creates within us "a truly wise and discerning vision of reality, as God sees it" (*VD*, 87). Through our renewal in Christ, we see differently. We were blind, but now we see by the light of faith.

On the left side of the chart, instruct students to write what they didn't see before about their lives or the world. On the right side, have them write what they now see differently because of what they learned in class and through their encounter with Christ.

Some students stumble over the word "covet" in the ninth and tenth commandments. During your lessons, help them understand what "covet" means with many real-life examples. Then, through a guided meditation, students can identify the people and things they covet for themselves. Through prayer and meditation, they will likely see how these desires are leading them into temptation and sin. A prayerful recitation of the Lord's Prayer after a meditation on these covetous desires can lead them away from such thoughts. Now they can use a Blind and See T-Chart to list the covetous feelings they didn't realize they had before and the way they see (or want to see) those people and objects differently now that they have experienced God's mercy.

STOP-DOING LIST

We have all heard of to-do lists. You write down a list of things you need to do for the day and then check them off as you accomplish each task. There is a growing trend to make the opposite kind of list: a stop-doing list or a not-to-do list. This includes a list of tasks or projects you should put aside so that you can focus your time, thoughts, and energy on more important projects. It is not that those things are bad; it is just that you want to focus on what is most important.

Likewise, your students may have a list of things that they feel called to stop doing. Through contemplation they can realize a change in priorities. Writing down a list of specific things not to do can help them commit to that change going forward. They can challenge themselves to avoid either the sins they were engaged in or the actions that lead them away from Christ and the person they feel called to be. The contemplation of the Ten Commandments in this activity may be obvious. Ask the students to list the specific ways they feel called to stop breaking the commandments they have learned about in your lesson.

A TRASH CAN PRAYER SERVICE

In the context of what you are teaching, have your students write down that list of things they need to stop doing, their sins, or the description of their old selves. In a lesson on the Ten Commandments, for example, they can write down how they have broken the commandments. Lead them in an Act of Contrition, making sure they are fully aware of the words they are reciting. Finally, tell the students to crumble up that piece of paper and, one by one, throw it in the trash.

The students know the changes they need to make, and they can experience a form of God's mercy by letting go of the sinful ways that are going in the trash. It may sound silly, but that physical act and expression of letting go of those sins can be a genuine experience of God's mercy. I distinctly remember the first time I did this activity in class and the unexpected tears I saw on the face of one of my students. Tears or no tears, that class walked away from the activity renewed, knowing that they can let go of actions, sins, and characteristics that God is calling them to change.

A CONVERSION COMMITMENT CARD

What new people are the students going to strive to become? How do they see themselves in a new way now that they have experienced this lesson and encountered Christ in some meaningful way? Again, the process of writing down this change can be motivational.

Help your students commit to the changes they know they need to make. Create for them a pledge card that reads something like "I, _____ [name], pledge to _____ by _____." For example, "I, John Doe, pledge to keep holy the Lord's Day by waking up early and asking my parents to drive me to Mass on Sunday." This pledge may not guarantee they will change, but it puts them in the right mindset to truly live out the conversion they want to see within themselves.

RECEIVING GOD'S GRACES

Now that your students recognize the changes they need to make, they shouldn't feel alone in the pursuit of a new way of life. God bestows on them his grace, the gift of his life, to help them live the life they are called to live. This means he bestows on them certain gifts of the Holy Spirit or virtues to help them be who they are truly meant to be.

Help the students identify these gifts or virtues, acknowledging that God is their source. There are a few creative ways to help them identify and embrace these graces. They can write an imaginary letter from God or a thank-you note to God identifying a specific grace and thanking him for bestowing it upon them. Or you can give them a printout of a blank gift card and tell them to write in it the name of the gift or virtue (or give them real, expired gift cards and invite them to label the cards with the gifts God is giving them).

In a lesson on the Ten Commandments, you can give the students a list of the commandments and a list of the cardinal virtues or gifts of the Holy Spirit. Work with them to match up the gifts and virtues with the commandments. Then, after some prayerful meditation on which of the commandments they struggle with the most, invite your students to pray for one of the gifts or virtues that will help them obey God's commands. Writing a letter to God or creating a keepsake to remind them of this gift will help them remember the need for God's help in seeking to change.

CONTEMPLATIVE JOURNAL

We can always go back to a standard journal practice, giving the students a question or thought to contemplate at the end of the lesson. Here are some journal prompts that might inspire your students to contemplate the conversion God is asking of them:

- What conversion of the mind, heart, and life is the Lord asking of me?

- What changes do I feel called to make in my life?

- What do I need to stop doing in order to be the person God calls me to be?

- How do I see myself or God differently today?

- How can I be more like Christ?

FROM CONTEMPLATION TO ACTION

Contemplation is an end in itself, not a means to an end. Its goal is not to bring about change. Its goal is unity—communion and intimacy with Jesus Christ. That is enough to hope for with our students.

Nevertheless, the natural effect of an encounter with Christ is action. Students who have met Jesus through meditation and prayer start to see themselves as Christ sees them. They start to see how they are being called to think and act differently. They start to see how they must live their lives in new ways.

In the next chapter we will discuss how you can help your students act differently as a result of their encounters with Christ. While you cannot control or grade these actions, you can certainly prompt the students to see how they can live in new ways after their experiences of contemplative prayer and reflection.

5 ACT
How Will I Make My Life a Gift for Others?

The process of lectio divina bears fruit in the way we live. We come to know God through lectio. We come to love God through meditatio, oratio, and contemplatio. Finally, we come to serve God through actio. Pope Benedict XVI wrote in *Verbum Domini*, "Lectio divina is not concluded until it arrives in action (*actio*), which moves the believer to make his or her life a gift for others in charity" (87). Your students must go forth from your lessons inspired by an encounter with Christ to change the way they relate to others.

In the last chapter, we focused on Jesus' frequent reminder that "whoever seeks to preserve his life will lose it, but whoever loses it will save it" (Lk 17:33). This exact passage inspired my favorite quote from the Second Vatican Council: "Man . . . cannot fully find himself except through a sincere gift of self" (*Gaudium et Spes*, 24). This final, actio step is all about helping students make a sincere gift of themselves in charity to others.

Think of this final step in your lesson preparation as unassigned and ungraded homework. You want your students to freely choose to act differently because of an encounter with Christ, not to do something to earn a grade or even your approval. Out of an experience of true encounter with Christ, you hope that they are compelled by the love of God to love one another as well.

Through this action step, you help students think of ways they can live differently. You help them recognize and prepare for the changes they wish to see in their lives. Living as a disciple of Christ is not easy, and when they commit to change, they will absolutely be challenged in their convictions. Therefore, to assist in the process of action, guide your students toward concrete applications of what they have learned and support them in their spiritual journey toward greater communion with Christ and others.

When speaking about contemplation, I introduced the idea of penance as connected to metanoia, or conversion. Penance is given by the priest during the sacrament of Reconciliation not to punish or somehow pay for a sin but as a way to express the change in one's heart—to show outwardly that one has turned back to God. St. John Paul II defined penance as "a conversion that passes from the heart to deeds and then to the Christian's whole life" (*Reconciliatio et Paenitentia*, 4). When you encourage students to practice action, it is like the priest giving a penitent his penance. The deed flows out of the call to conversion and, we hope, spills over into a new way of living.

THE CULTURE OF ENCOUNTER

Another way of looking at action compared to contemplation is to think of the two ways recent popes have used the word "encounter." Pope Benedict XVI popularized the use of the phrase "encounter with Christ" in a particular way in his encyclical *Deus Caritas Est*: "Being Christian is not the result of an ethical choice or a lofty idea, but the encounter with an event, a person, which gives life a new horizon and a decisive direction" (1).

Pope Francis highlighted the importance of this passage in his apostolic exhortation *Evangelii Gaudium*, writing, "I never tire of repeating those words of Benedict XVI which take us to the very heart of the Gospel" (7). He further frames the importance of encountering Christ by challenging Christians to embrace their call to be missionary disciples: "Every

Christian is a missionary to the extent that he or she has encountered the love of God in Christ Jesus: we no longer say that we are 'disciples' and 'missionaries,' but rather that we are 'missionary disciples'" (*EG*, 120).

Action, therefore, flows out of contemplation. Having experienced an encounter with Christ, your students can go forth as missionary disciples to share that encounter with others. This is the heart of evangelization, and it does not require anyone to be a preacher. Pope Francis frequently refers to another way of thinking about encounter: the encounter with others. "Whenever we encounter another person in love, we learn something new about God. Whenever our eyes are opened to acknowledge the other, we grow in the light of faith and knowledge of God" (*EG*, 272).

Pope Francis speaks of a "culture of encounter" in which we do not close ourselves off from others but instead connect more deeply with them. He uses this phrase so often that it is somewhat difficult to directly define. He uses it to promote relationship over individualism. He uses it in reference to world peace as he did in his Super Bowl video in 2017. "The culture of encounter means recognizing that we are all children of God, despite our differences," he once tweeted. Just as we are silent and attentive during meditation and contemplation, we are also called to be silent and listen to others, seeing God in each one of them.

Your students, therefore, are called to encounter Christ and, out of that constant encounter, to feel compelled to share the love they have experienced with others. It starts with an encounter with Christ but flows into an encounter with others. The more successful you are in teaching your students to contemplate through an encounter with Christ, the more they can offer that love to others who need it the most. There is, however, a difference between wanting to change and changing. To turn intention into action, your students must identify specific situations in which they can live out the change they want to see in themselves. For this chapter, imagine how you can encourage action through lessons focused on the liturgical year, especially Advent and Lent.

WRITTEN PLAN OF ACTION

On a blank sheet of paper or a graphic organizer you have designed, ask your students to write down a plan of action for how they will live out what God is calling them to be and do. This can be a simple list of the specific places and times in which they need to act differently than they would have before the lesson. Just the act of writing down these opportunities for action will trigger a reminder of the way the students want to change in the moment in which they need it. Here are a few ways to design this Plan of Action sheet:

I Will/I Will Not: Direct students to create two columns on a piece of loose-leaf paper. On the left tell them to list a series of "I will . . ." statements and on the right a series of "I will not . . ." statements. During Lent, for example, what will they add ("I will . . .") in terms of prayer and almsgiving? What will they give up as a form of fasting ("I will not . . .")?

Scenes: Focus on situations in which your students encounter opportunities for action. Invite them to draw pictures of scenes in which they are treating others with love specifically in the way they feel called to do at the end of the lesson. In a lesson on Lent, for example, they can draw a picture of themselves in the lunch line on a Friday saying "no thank you" to the offering of pepperoni pizza.

People: Ask the students to identify specific people they feel called to serve in a particular way and then to list the ways they will help these individuals. Almsgiving is a difficult concept to teach to kids who don't have any income of their own to give. So resolving to help specific people in specific ways is a good way to apply the idea of almsgiving to their lives.

SCENARIO DISCUSSIONS

Another way to help students prepare for action is to describe for them a moral dilemma or scenario that requires a choice of action. If you craft these scenarios to resemble situations that students may actually encounter, the discussion in class about these situations can have a strong impact.

Students can think through all the possible ways to act and use what they have learned about God and themselves to plan the correct course of action. The discussion alone will improve their decision making later when confronting similar situations.

For your Lenten lesson, direct the students to make a list of things they feel called to give up during Lent, then make a list of scenarios in which they will be especially tempted or challenged to forget their commitment. Discuss them as a class and work with the students to come up with the best ways to overcome those challenges.

SKITS

Take the scenario discussion one step further and lead the students in a skit acting out a problematic situation. Most kids enjoy the skits, and they understand the details of the scenario better when acted out. Skits also give the students the chance to put themselves in someone else's shoes. Either by acting or by observing, they can consider who they might act like in that situation.

Let's say your lesson on Lent focuses on the importance of praying more throughout the day. Divide your students into groups and assign each moment of the day to one of the groups. Give them a graphic organizer or sheet of paper to brainstorm the obstacles to praying during these times, then invite them to plan a short skit to act out those obstacles with the main character in the skit overcoming them to add prayer to his day.

THE ART OF ACCOMPANIMENT

Another concept Pope Francis and the Church's bishops have emphasized is the art of accompaniment. Here is how I defined the art of accompaniment in my book *To Heal, Proclaim, and Teach*:

> Essentially, the art of accompaniment is about listening with openness. Rather than

> just listening to someone during a conversation, we ask questions about what our friend is saying and seek to find out what is really behind the words he says. In response, we open up our hearts and allow ourselves to experience a compassionate closeness that is required for a genuine spiritual encounter.
>
> The goal of the art of accompaniment is to open up and be a person whom someone can confide in rather than seeking to find a solution to someone's problem. (155)

To achieve this goal of accompaniment, you must go beyond mere classroom instruction. You must not only teach and inspire but also walk with your students and help them turn intention into action. Essentially, you must act as a mentor to your students throughout the year. Here are a few suggestions for doing this:

Between the Bells: The time between the bells before or after class can be just as important as the time you spend with students in class. Those few minutes give you the chance to be a fellow disciple and not just a teacher. You can get to know the students better and increase your awareness about what is going on in their lives. You can help them make connections between their lives and your lessons during this time, but try not to force those conversations. The best thing to do between classes is listen. Students, like all of us, want to be heard.

Journal Notes: If you have a regular journal practice in class, the feedback and notes you write can have an impact on the students as they strive to change into the image that God is calling them to. Write supportive comments. Encourage them. Praise the plans they have in place to apply what they are learning. During the season of Advent, for example, encourage their plans and attempts to prepare for Christmas in prayer and action.

Personal Prayer: In your prayers for your students, focus on their specific stories and the struggles they are going through right now. Personalize your prayer intentions. The more you know about what is going on in their lives, the more you know what to pray about. Take a class list home and pray for the students one by one. Think of the particular ways in which the lesson you are now preparing inspires the intentions you have for each student. This prayer practice will incline you to check in more often with the students individually so you know how to pray for them. Telling them you are praying for them about a specific challenge encourages them, too.

Accompaniment, however, doesn't have to be your responsibility alone. It is also something you can encourage the students to do for one another. Try the following ways to help students practice the art of accompaniment.

Prayer Partners: For the entire year, semester, or quarters of the year, pair up students as prayer partners. Arrange for them to meet regularly to ask each other to pray about things going on in their lives. You can even build a prayer partner meeting into your lessons to ensure that they have some accountability for whatever action steps they feel they need to take as a result of the lesson.

Small Groups: Expanding the partner idea a little further, set aside time for the students to meet regularly in small groups of four to six students. Encourage them to share prayer requests in the group and give them the chance to check in with one another regularly. You can even make small-group time a regular practice at the end of your lesson to give students the opportunity to work out a plan of action to apply what they have learned and experienced in class.

These opportunities for accompaniment and support aren't just nice to do; they are essential for a life of discipleship. Remember, Jesus sent out the disciples two by two, not alone. He chose a group of apostles to go out to proclaim the Good News. Even St. Paul traveled with fellow disciples and often wrote to support them in doing the work of God.

ACTION HOMEWORK ASSIGNMENTS

For each lesson, think of some ideas for action you can suggest to the students before they go. These suggestions give you something to talk about on an ongoing basis with your students, checking in frequently to see how they are doing in living out what they have learned. Following are a few ideas, but come up with your own suggestions tailored to the students as much as possible.

Random Acts of Kindness: I can remember my grade school hosting a Random Acts of Kindness Week. The idea was to do something kind and unplanned for someone who needed help. The concept increases our awareness of the needs of those around us and encourages us to be kind in a spontaneous way. You can apply this concept to your lessons. At the end of a lesson on Lent and giving alms, for example, you might suggest that the students be prepared to give money to someone in need sometime in the future. They may not have an immediate opportunity, but they can look out for their chance in the weeks of Lent.

An X-Day Challenge: Participating in a thirty-day challenge has become common among self-help advocates and health seekers. It is a good way to get motivated and make exercise or self-care a habit. You can apply this concept to class as well. The challenge can last for one month, one week, or an entire liturgical season (four weeks, forty days, fifty days, etc.). You can attach actions to traditional devotional prayers such as novenas (nine days) or Marian consecration (thirty-three days). You can provide students with an Advent calendar, for example, with a single goal or different suggestions for taking action during the Advent season. Again, the key is to make sure the actions you suggest align with your lesson. The challenge should be motivated by your students' new understanding of the ideas you have taught them and the experience of encounter with Christ they had in class.

Prayers of Petition: While prayer may not feel very active, the intention to give oneself in love and charity can be appropriately fulfilled through prayer. After experiencing your lesson, for whom should the students feel compelled to pray? During Advent, who is looking for Christ to come into their life?

During Christmas, who needs to experience Christ's presence? During Lent, who is carrying a cross that they can share in prayer? During Easter, who is in need of the joy of the Resurrection?

LEARN, LOVE, AND LIVE

You have the opportunity to teach your students for only a short time. You teach them for a year, sometimes more, and then they go on to the next person who will help them grow in their faith. You may never see them again. It is difficult to think about, but it is true. You are planting seeds that you pray will bear fruit years later into their adulthood. The Christian author John C. Maxwell once wrote, "Success each day should be judged by the seeds sown, not the harvest reaped" (*The Difference Maker*, 178). You may not be the one to harvest the fruits of your labors, but the hope is clear. You want your students to live lives of service to others.

To prepare them to live out their faith one day as adults, taking action to serve God and their neighbors, you have to concentrate on both the head and the heart. You cannot hope for a good harvest with the head alone. Understanding of ideas does not necessarily lead to a relationship with Christ. You must not, on the other hand, seek only to influence the emotions of the heart. Over time those feelings fade, and the firm foundation of faith is lost. Instead, lead your students to learn about and love the Lord. Help them think with their heads and reflect with their hearts. Invite them into a relationship through an encounter with the living God. Out of those experiences, mere seeds planted in their souls, pray that they will live in loving service of God and others.

I pray that as you apply the steps and strategies in this book, your students will learn about who God is and what he desires to teach them. They will learn about his love for them. They will enter into a loving encounter with the Lord through meditation, prayer, and contemplation. They will experience his love and love him back. Holding fast to that love, they will go forth and live new lives of humility loving others as Christ has loved them. They will know God with their heads, love God with their hearts, and serve God with their actions.

CONCLUSION

Questions, Suggestions, and Best Practices

I want to conclude by addressing some of the questions that may arise as you integrate the lectio divina approach into the way you teach. I hope you open this book again and again, returning to it for ideas and inspiration. This section will help you get the most out of the book and the unique approach that it advocates.

SHOULD I USE THE FIVE LECTIO DIVINA STEPS AS THE TEMPLATE FOR MY LESSON PLAN?

While you can certainly use the five lectio divina steps (lectio, meditatio, oratio, contemplatio, and actio) to outline a lesson plan, I suggest instead that you apply the steps to the way you already teach. Think of the steps in this book more as a checklist than a template. You may cycle through the learn and meditate steps multiple times before coming to the prayer step. If I were applying this approach to my lessons for the first time, for example, I would look at how I open my lessons. I am a big advocate for giving students bell work assignments (see pages 39–40). Just because bell work is at the beginning of class, however, doesn't mean that it has to focus on the learning step alone. These assignments can encourage meditation or be opportunities for students to pray or contemplate. They can also be invitations to journal about actions they have taken to apply what they learned in class to their everyday lives.

Think of the last lesson that you planned. Or, if you have the lesson plan written out, go back through it and write L, M, O, C, and A next to the parts that align with each of the steps. You will probably find some steps occur out of order. The first thing you do may be a meditation or a prayer, or you may find that you don't spend enough time on meditation. That is OK as long as the main topic you are introducing follows the steps in order.

As you apply this approach, you will see the need to follow the basic structure of the steps when introducing new ideas. Meditation is difficult without first clarifying the meaning of the things that you teach. Once students fully grasp what something means, they can meditate on what it means to them. Likewise, the prayer experience you plan in class will have the most impact if it follows a personal meditation. Contemplative prayer will be more directly related to the lesson if it follows the previous three steps, and action will be more focused as well.

Now think ahead to your next lesson. As you plan, make sure you dedicate time to each one of the lectio divina steps. Consider the following questions:

- Are you setting aside the necessary time to build connections between what students know now and the new ideas you are introducing? (Lectio)

- Are you giving the students time to make personal connections between these ideas and their everyday lives? (Meditatio)

- Do you give them the opportunity to pray in response to God after making these connections? (Oratio)

- Are you planning opportunities for contemplative personal time between God and the students? (Contemplatio)

- Do you help them plan for and consider how they will share what they have learned and experienced with others? (Actio)

Every time you plan a lesson, look back over what you prepared and label each section with an L, M, O, C, or A. Make sure the heart of your lesson progresses from lectio (head) to more prayerful, heartfelt experiences of the mysteries of faith (meditatio, oratio, contemplatio, actio). If any of the elements are missing, go back in and add something to your lesson to focus on that step.

WHAT IF I RUN OUT OF TIME BEFORE WE COMPLETE EACH LECTIO DIVINA STEP?

It might take longer to teach students a given idea than you anticipated. You might find yourself trying to squeeze in meditation and prayer time at the very end of your lesson before the class is over. You probably already feel the pressure of having more to teach than you can possibly fit into one lesson.

First of all, forgive yourself for not teaching everything. Textbooks and curricula include more than you can possibly teach in a given year. You are only planting seeds in hope that the next year someone else will continue the work and nurture what you have planted. For the ideas to bear fruit in your students' lives, however, you have to help them make personal connections. You cannot fall into the trap of just teaching ideas and information. Your students will slowly drift away.

Your primary goal as a religious educator is an encounter, not an education. Are you educating the students? Yes, absolutely, but you are called to do so much more. You must also dedicate the time necessary to create opportunities for encounter. Sometimes that means pushing your meditation, prayer, and contemplation activities to the next time you meet. Sometimes that means teaching a lot less during class than you feel like you should. The point is to always touch *both* the head and the heart. Sacrifice something you want them to learn to give yourself time to guide them in meditation and prayer about what you plan to teach.

HOW DO I GRADE MEDITATION, PRAYER, AND CONTEMPLATION ASSIGNMENTS? OR SHOULD I GRADE THEM?

If you are a religion teacher in a Catholic school, then you have to record grades based on effort and performance in class. When I was teaching religion in a Catholic school, some students (and parents) objected to my rigorous grading of their work and effort. I wasn't grading any differently than teachers

in other subject areas. In a Catholic school, religion/
theology is an academic subject just as important as
the other classes students are taking.

Grades should be a measure of mastery. If students master the lectio part of the lesson, they should
be able to demonstrate this in the assessments you
use to assign grades. A poor performance on an
assessment is feedback for the student to continue
to improve and master the material.

Grades, however, should also be a reflection of
effort. Students show effort by completing assignments as asked. Clear instructions and rubrics communicate expectations to the students. They should
be able to meet those expectations through hard
work. While your students can't show you mastery
of knowledge in their meditation and prayer assignments, they can certainly show you effort. As long
as the grades are used as feedback to improve effort,
you can assign grades to meditation and prayer
assignments. Just be clear about what the grade is
for. You are not measuring their ability to pray; you
are measuring the effort they put into meeting your
expectations for the assignment.

WHAT IS THE BEST WAY TO USE TECHNOLOGY IN A LECTIO DIVINA LESSON?

Technology will not solve your teaching challenges. Use what you know how to use best. There are benefits, sure, but also dangers when it comes to modern technology. The way I like to frame educational technology was inspired by Jim Collins in his book *Good to Great*. He described technology as an accelerator: "When used right, technology becomes an accelerator of momentum, not a creator of it" (152).

Technology is an accelerator, not the answer to your problems. Start with the simplest forms of technology and get a handle on the techniques described in this book before adding a new level of technology to help. Think about technology in a more rudimentary way. Paper is a form of technology. Books and paper are an advancement over the previous method for copying and sharing ideas—writing in scrolls and on papyrus. Whether you use paper, papyrus, or digital technology, the most important thing is how you use them, not what you use.

Will multimedia help with meditation? Video, audio, and interactive media can make meditation more meaningful or more distracting, depending on how you have prepared your students. If you show a video or play a recording in class, make sure to set up what the students will watch or listen to ahead of time. Give them very specific ways to personally relate to the media just as you would for a meditation on a text. As much as possible, remove distracting links to other videos, songs, apps, or websites. Keep them entirely focused on the single source of meditation. If students have devices in their hands, be sure to give good reasons for them to single-task and focus on your activity so that the many distractions on the devices don't interrupt their flow and direct their attention away from meditation and prayer.

HOW DO I DO LECTIO DIVINA OF SCRIPTURE WITHIN A LECTIO DIVINA LESSON?

Since this book has focused on applying lectio divina to lesson planning, we haven't discussed how to guide students through a self-contained lectio divina process applied to sacred scripture (its original purpose). I recommend frequent use of lectio divina in reading scripture, too, as part of your overall lesson. You can guide students through the steps all at once rather than spread them out through an entire lesson.

Lectio: First, hand out individual Bibles to your students to read in class. Pick a passage and do some prereading with them by identifying difficult words, names, and places that need to be explained. Give the students a mini-lesson to help them understand the context of the passage, then read the passage together.

Meditatio: Next, invite them to search their minds and hearts for their own stories, thoughts, worries, and emotions that relate to this passage. What similar experiences have they had in the past? What similar situations are they in now? What future situations will they encounter similar to what they read about? Guide them to imagine themselves as bystanders in the story or to put themselves in the situation of one of the people in the story. Then, bridge the gap between the story and their personal lives. From here the students can ask themselves what God is saying to them through this passage. Rereading the passage will help open them up to the Spirit, who will reveal these conclusions to them.

Oratio: Once the students experience some clarity about God's will for them through meditation, they can respond to God in prayer. They can offer petitions asking for forgiveness or help. They can give God thanks or praise and bless him for his presence in their lives. Find an appropriate prayer or give them the chance to visualize a conversation with Christ with spontaneous prayer.

Contemplatio: Ask the students to reflect on the person they are to become after reading this passage. Give them a moment to silently recognize the presence of Christ in his Word.

Actio: From this moment of connection with Christ, the students can prepare for how they can apply this experience to their daily lives. They can think ahead to situations in which they will act differently now that they have encountered Christ in his Word.

WHAT IS THE BEST WAY TO DO LECTIO DIVINA WITH YOUNGER CHILDREN?

Just because lectio divina has a fancy Latin name doesn't mean you have to be old and mature to do it. Children can practice each of the steps just as well as older students and adults, only a little differently. My hope is that you will adapt the suggestions in this book in ways that will work best for your students. Each lectio divina step is available for anyone to encounter Christ. Nevertheless, here are a few ways to adapt each step to younger ages.

Lectio: Teaching for understanding is all about connecting what someone knows to a new idea. This doesn't mean dumbing things down for little kids. It means using analogies, metaphors, and the Seven Scaffolding Strategies to connect what you are teaching to what they already understand. Don't talk for too long, and try not to use more than one specific way to explain something. From here you can transition into a more personal experience of the lesson.

Meditation: Kids love to talk about themselves. Share any story in class and three kids will soon have hands raised while they blurt out how something similar (or something seemingly irrelevant) happened to them. The challenge in meditation, therefore, is channeling that energy to share and connect to personal memories related to the specific topic you are teaching. Help the students to make connections between those memories and life events and what you are teaching. It may take more work to process the memories and make connections, so be sure to use graphic organizers with opportunities to draw the memories and make connections visually, especially for preliterate children.

Prayers: Find simple prayers to teach to the students and help them see how those prayers connect to their memories in the meditation. If possible, get their little bodies moving with hand motions and physical expressions of the prayer. They are forced to sit so often and for so long that young children need opportunities to move around. Expressing prayers with movement is a good way to do that.

Contemplation: Can kids really contemplate? Remember St. Teresa's description of contemplation as a close sharing between friends. There is no need to complicate contemplation. Give the kids some silent time to visualize the Lord. Engage the senses with images, statues, bells, smells, and anything else that will help the students step away from the class and into a heightened focus on the Lord. Then, help them think ahead to how they are called to convert. What does God want them to say and do differently in their lives?

Action: Be specific. Help them think about one situation in which they can apply what they have learned. Check in with them the next time you meet to see how they did. Often, you won't have to remind them because they will be ready to share next time they see you. Be the support to make those intentions a reality, often checking in and reminding them what they can do to live what they learn.

SHOULD I GO THROUGH THE LECTIO DIVINA PROCESS MYSELF IN PREPARATION FOR EACH LESSON?

Pope Francis advised priests to prayerfully prepare their homilies in his document on evangelization:

> There is one particular way of listening to what the Lord wishes to tell us in his word and of letting ourselves be transformed by the Spirit. It is what we call lectio divina. It consists of reading God's word in a moment of prayer and allowing it to enlighten and renew us. This prayerful reading of the Bible is not something separate from the study undertaken by the preacher to ascertain the central message of the text; on the contrary, it should begin with that study and then go on to discern how that same message speaks to his own life. (*EG*, 152)

Prepare each lesson with a similar approach, going through each step of lectio divina yourself. What is the most important thing to understand in this lesson? What is God saying to me through this lesson? What can I say in response? Standing before Christ as his teacher and servant, in what ways am I called to change and grow? How can I give myself in charity to my students in this lesson?

Go through the activities, exercises, and meditations you plan to use in class. Experience an encounter with Christ yourself. Out of that encounter you can better encounter Christ in the kids that you teach. You can authentically guide them as a fellow disciple on the journey toward God.

I will conclude with this one last insight, something I come back to again and again in my thoughts about our work in religious education. In his document on evangelization, *Evangelii Nuntiandi*, Pope Paul VI wrote that "modern man listens more willingly to witnesses than to teachers, and if he does listen to teachers, it is because they are witnesses" (41). Be Christ's witness. You are more than just a teacher. Be the bridge between your students and Christ. Guide them with confidence to encounter Christ, knowing that the relationship you have with God can be shared with others. God wants to know your students intimately. Knowing what he is like is not enough. He wants them to know that he loves them. He wants them to experience that love. Show those students how God loves you and give them hope that he loves them, too.

The year I realized I was teaching my Confirmation students to know about God and the Church's teachings without showing them how to love God was the year I realized I was just a teacher, not a witness. I was good at instruction but bad at intimacy. Those confirmandi didn't know why their catechist loved the Lord. They didn't know how the gifts of the Holy Spirit had influenced his life. As a result, Christ was just a concept and not someone they could encounter in real life.

I no longer teach that way. Today, I strive to be a witness more than a teacher. I try to be a disciple more than a teacher. I recognize that above all else, our students need to encounter Christ in the classroom with both their heads and their hearts. I hope that in reading this book, you feel the same way I do. He is the center of our work in religious education. We listen to him and we seek to see him in everything we do. May your life be an example of how to encounter the risen Lord everywhere, starting in your classroom.